Weetabix

Book of the

MILLENNIUM

Volume 1: 1001–1350

from the publishers of
The **HUTCHINSON**
ENCYCLOPEDIA

Helicon

First published for Weetabix Limited in Great Britain in 1999 by
Helicon Publishing Ltd
42 Hythe Bridge Street
Oxford OX1 2EP
e-mail address: admin@helicon.co.uk
Web site: http://www.helicon.co.uk

The Weetabix name and logo are the registered trade marks of Weetabix Limited.

Typesetting by Tech Type, Abingdon, Oxon
Layout and design by Norton Matrix Limited, Bath
Printed in Italy by De Agostini, Novara
ISBN: 1-85986-325-6

British Library Cataloguing in Publication Data

A catalogue record for this book is available from the British Library.

Papers used by Helicon Publishing Ltd are natural recyclable products
made from wood grown in sustainable forests. The manufacturing
processes of both raw material and paper conform to the environmental
regulations of the country of origin.

Contributors and Advisors

Ian Crofton	Susan Mendelsohn
Bernadette Crowley	Nigel Seaton
Susan Cuthbert	Cath Senker
Giles Hastings	Andrew Solway
Maggy Hendry	Lisa Sullivan
Louise Jones	Sarah Wearne
Brenda Lofthouse	Christine Withers

Editorial and Production

Editorial Director
Hilary McGlynn

Managing Editor
Katie Emblen

Project Managers
Robert Snedden
Lisa Sullivan

Editors
Rachel Minay
Edith Summerhayes

Production
Tony Ballsdon

Picture Research
Elizabeth Loving

Cartography
Olive Pearson

Art and Design
Terence Caven

Contents

Weetabix

Book of the
MILLENNIUM
Volume 1: 1001–1350

from the publishers of
The HUTCHINSON
ENCYCLOPEDIA

The World 1001–1350

about 1000
Leif Ericsson sails from Greenland and reaches North America.

1066
William the Conqueror succeeds in the Norman conquest of England at the Battle of Hastings.

about 1100
The Anasazi people, the ancestors of the Pueblo Native American tribes, build houses in the stone cliffs.

14th century
The Shona people begin building the massive stone buildings of Great Zimbabwe.

1347
The Black Death reaches Europe from Asia.

13th century
Genghis Khan and his grandson Kublai greatly expand the Mongol empire across most of Asia.

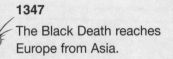

1192
Minamoto Yoritomo is the first *shogun* in Japan.

1113
The Khmer begin building the great temple of Angkor Wat in Cambodia.

1095
Pope Urban II launches the First Crusade to regain the Holy Land.

about 1000
Maoris from Polynesia settle in New Zealand.

Viking Expeditions

Who Were the Vikings?

The Vikings came from Scandinavia during the period from 800 to 1100. Some came from Norway, some from Sweden, and some from Denmark. They were great travellers and sailed to other parts of Europe, where they traded, raided, and often settled. Using their long, narrow ships they were able to travel inland on rivers to take gold and land. They were fierce warriors, and by the end of the 11th century they occupied lands as far apart as North America and central Russia.

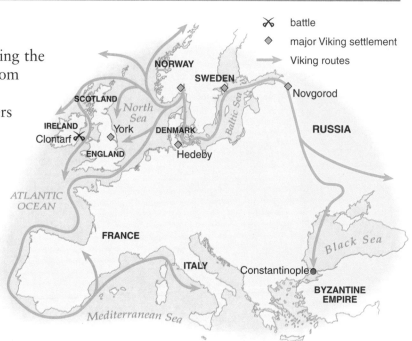

The voyages of the Norwegians.

At home the Vikings had an organized government system. People in local areas voted at assemblies, called 'things', which made laws and held trials for criminals. The Vikings loved storytelling, and poets, or 'skalds', would tell of the adventures of Norse heroes or legends of their gods, such as Thor, god of the sky. Later, these stories were written down and called 'sagas'.

By the year 1000, Vikings already occupied lands in what are now England, Scotland, Ireland, France, Russia, Iceland, and Greenland. Viking traders sailed down the rivers of Russia and across the Black Sea as far as Constantinople (modern Istanbul in

Shipbuilding

The Vikings were expert shipbuilders. Longships, used for fishing and raiding, carried them tremendous distances across stormy seas. Their hulls were very shallow so they could sail up rivers and land on beaches. Their long, curved prows were carved into dragons' heads to scare their enemies.

The fine detail on this ship's weathervane shows the skill of the Viking metalworkers.

The Travels of Leif Ericsson

Leif Ericsson was the son of Eric the Red, who had travelled to Greenland and began a Viking settlement there in around 986. In around 1000, Leif and a crew of 35 men set sail from this settlement, called Osterbygd, on the west coast of Greenland. They finally reached North America and explored three sites, which Leif named Helluland (thought to be Baffin Island), Markland (thought to be Labrador), and Vinland. People think that Vinland might have been in present-day Newfoundland. In 1963 archaeologists found ruins of a Viking settlement at L'Anse-aux-Meadows on the northern tip of Newfoundland, and these ruins match Leif's description.

Canute (ruled 1016–1035)

Canute II (known as 'the Great') was born in around 995, the son of Sweyn Forkbeard, King of the Danes. Canute conquered England in 1013, and when his father died the following year Canute's warriors named him king of England. He fought against the armies of Ethelred, the English king, and in 1015 took over all of England except London. When Ethelred died in 1016 the Londoners named his son, Edmund II, king. Edmund's army fought against Canute and was defeated at Ashingdon, Essex, in October. When Edmund died the following month, Canute became the undisputed king.

Canute was a wise ruler and managed to establish peace with the English and other European powers. To help achieve this, he married the widow of King Ethelred, Emma of Normandy. He became the ruler of Denmark in 1018 and of Norway in 1028. He died in 1035. His two sons reigned after him, but after the last of them died in 1042, an English king, Edward the Confessor, was restored to the throne.

Turkey), the capital of the Byzantine Empire. Some Vikings even formed the Varangian Guard, the personal bodyguard of the emperor. The Vikings had a great effect on the laws, customs, and language in the places they settled. For example, English place names ending in '-by', such as Whitby and Grimsby, are from the Norse word for 'castle'.

The Vikings Defeated in Ireland

Vikings from Norway began attacks on Ireland in 795, and the Irish fought to drive them out for more than 200 years. Finally, in 1014, the Irish won an important victory at the Battle of Clontarf, near Dublin. The sons of Brian Boru, the Irish king, led the Irish army. The king, who had been fighting the Vikings since he was a teenager, was too old to fight himself. He was waiting for news of the battle when he was killed in his tent by a Viking intruder. Nevertheless, the victory meant the end of Viking dominance in Ireland.

The Last Viking Conquest

Perhaps the most famous Viking victory was in 1066 at the Battle of Hastings. These Vikings were called Normans ('northmen'). They had been given Normandy by the king of France in 911 to persuade them to stop their raids on his country. Since then the Normans had adopted the language and culture of France, but still had the old Viking spirit of adventure. In the battle, William, Duke of Normandy, defeated the English king, Harold, and shortly afterwards William took the throne of England.

Rise of the Normans

Who Were the Normans?

The Normans lived in northern France, in an area called Normandy. Their dress, language, and customs were French, but they were not French. They were descended from Vikings, or 'Northmen', from Scandinavia.

From around AD800 the Vikings sailed from Scandinavia in their longships to terrorize and kill people and seize their goods and gold. In 911, a Viking chief, Rollo (about 860–932), made an agreement with the French king. In return for some French land, Rollo and his people would protect France against attack, even from other Vikings.

Rollo and his people rapidly developed a strong society in Normandy, with many firm rules and regulations. The Normans adopted many aspects of French culture and civilization and became Christians. Rollo's great-great-great-grandson was Duke William of Normandy.

Edward the Confessor, king of England. Edward was a very religious man and was made a saint by the Catholic Church after his death.

England before the Conquest

The reign of the English king Edward the Confessor (ruled 1042–1066) had been long and peaceful. He was admired for his commitment to Christianity, and this influenced his subjects. His grandfather, Ethelred, had been unable to keep the Danes from plundering the land and demanding huge sums of gold. Ethelred had been so weak and unpopular that England had been taken over by a series of Danish kings. Edward's reign was a relief, but England was unsettled. The country was divided into regions ruled by earls, powerful men, most of whom wanted more power. Harold, Earl of Wessex, became King Harold II after Edward's death in 1066, but there were other earls who might have caused him trouble if he had lived longer.

The Beginnings of the Conflict

It is said by some that in 1051 Edward the Confessor promised that Duke William of Normandy could be king after him. Edward was grateful for the protection he had received from the Normans as a little boy. He and his brother had been driven out of England by the Danish king, Canute. Canute, and then his sons, had ruled England from 1016 to 1042. Canute had wanted the English heirs to the throne out of the way, preferably dead.

In 1064 the English earl Harold of Wessex went to Normandy. On behalf of King Edward, he promised William the English throne and pledged his own support as well. But in 1066, when Edward died, Harold claimed that Edward had made him his successor and became king. William claimed that the English throne was rightfully his. With the backing of the Pope he invaded England at Pevensey and fought Harold at the Battle of Hastings.

The Early Years of William of Normandy (about 1027–1087)

William of Normandy was born in about 1027. His parents lived together as man and wife, but were not married, and in later years people often called him 'William the Bastard'. When his father, Duke Robert, died while on a pilgrimage to Jerusalem, the eight-year-old William became Duke of Normandy.

William's life was difficult. He did not know whom to trust – many people wanted him dead and plotted against him. But William was not defeated. He became strong, tough, and ruthless.

In 1053 William married Matilda of Flanders. Neighbouring rulers had opposed the match and so at first the Pope wouldn't allow it. William persisted and got his way. Their marriage was good and long-lasting, and they had nine or ten children.

A Norman church in the Cotswolds. Norman churches typically have low, square towers like this.

A Monk's View

Although the Normans were great soldiers and conquerors, not everybody admired them wholeheartedly. The Norman monk Geoffrey of Malaterra wrote about his fellow countrymen, and he said that they:

- were crafty and quick to take revenge
- were greedy for wealth and power
- liked to impress others and showed off their wealth, but were also mean and tight-fisted
- copied all kinds of things
- spoke well and persuasively, often getting their own way by flattery
- were immoral, so they had to be governed strictly
- were physically tough, easily putting up with hard work, cold, and hunger
- loved hunting and falconry and would dress grandly for these pursuits.

A Norman lord goes hunting with a falcon. This was a favourite hobby of the well-off Normans.

The Battle of Hastings

There was a great deal of work for blacksmiths to do before a battle, preparing weapons and shoes for horses.

One of the best-known dates in British history is 1066. This is the year of the invasion of William of Normandy. His victory at the Battle of Hastings led to Norman rule of England.

The Armies Take Position

On 13 October 1066 King Harold II positioned his English army of around 6,000 men on Senlac Hill. He had marched quickly from Stamford Bridge in Yorkshire.
The previous week he had had to fight the Norwegians who had tried to invade the country. Now he faced a new threat from Duke William of Normandy.
Senlac was a good defensive position 11 kilometres (7 miles) from Hastings, where William had remained with his invading army of Normans, French, and Bretons (men from Brittany).

Harold placed his men along the top of the hill forming a 'shield wall'. On the sides were the 'fyrdmen', the part-time soldiers, and in the centre were Harold's finest troops, the 'housecarls'.

William arrived at dawn on 14 October and placed his men at the bottom of the hill where he could clearly see Harold's personal banner, the Fighting Man, and also the Dragon of Wessex fluttering over the English centre.

The Battle

The battle began at about 9.00 a.m. when the Norman archers fired at the English. Then the foot soldiers advanced up the slope only to be met by fierce resistance from the whole English army. Having failed to break the English line

This section from the Bayeux Tapestry shows part of the Norman invasion fleet sailing to England.

William's mounted knights began their attack, but they too met with little success.

Attack followed attack until there was a near disaster for the Normans. The Bretons, on the left, began to flee and were chased by the fyrdmen. However, William managed to send some knights to encircle and cut down the English. The battle raged on until William tried tricking the English into thinking he was fleeing again. As the English chased the Normans, William's men surrounded them and killed many.

Rumour of William's Death

In the middle of the battle a rumour spread that William was dead. This nearly brought disaster down upon the Normans, but William quickly took off his helmet and is said to have shouted, 'I am still alive and with God's help I shall still win...' Seeing that their leader was not dead ended the panic in the Norman army.

With night fast approaching William told his archers to fire high into the air, raining arrows down

onto the centre of the English army around Harold. William then attacked Harold's position furiously. The Norman knights broke through, killing many of Harold's housecarls. Harold himself either died from an arrow in the eye, or was cut down during this final attack. With the king dead and the army leaderless, the English surrendered.

William Becomes King

William did not head for London immediately. He moved through the south, burning villages as he went. He crossed the Thames near Wallingford (now in Oxfordshire) and then arrived at Berkhamsted (now in Hertfordshire) where he was accepted as king by the remaining English noblemen. He was crowned on Christmas Day 1066 in Westminster Abbey.

A mounted cavalry charge against foot soldiers is shown in this scene from the Bayeux Tapestry.

How Do We Know About the Battle of Hastings?

The story of the battle has been put together using two main sources. Firstly, there are stories written by people who lived at the time. These are not very detailed, however, and the reports of the English and the Normans often contradict each other.

Perhaps more interesting is the Bayeux Tapestry. This is a 900-year-old strip of over 70 pictures, like a modern comic. It shows the events leading up to the battle, the battle itself, what the soldiers wore, what weapons they used, what the ships and buildings were like, and even what they ate.

9

The Norman Inheritance

1066 Battle of Hastings: Duke William of Normandy wins and becomes William I of England. Norman noblemen are given land that had belonged to the Anglo-Saxons (English). The Anglo-Saxons lose their power and the Normans become the English nobility. The feudal system is introduced. Norman (or Romanesque) architecture flourishes in Britain and Norman French becomes the language of the court and literature.

1071 William I defeats the last Anglo-Saxon rebel, Hereward the Wake.

1072 The Norman Robert Guiscard completes his conquest of southern Italy.

1082 Robert Guiscard takes the island of Corfu and defeats the Byzantine emperor at Durazzo, in Albania.

1085 Robert Guiscard dies.

1086 The Domesday Book is written.

1087 William I of England dies. His second son, William Rufus, becomes king as William II. William I's eldest son, Robert, becomes Duke of Normandy.

1091 The Norman Roger de Hauteville, brother of Robert Guiscard, captures Sicily, in southern Italy.

1096 Robert, Duke of Normandy, borrows money from William Rufus, 'lending' him Normandy in exchange, so that Robert can join the First Crusade.

1098 Prince Bohemond, son of Robert Guiscard, captures Antioch, in Turkey.

1100 William Rufus is killed. His brother Henry becomes king of England as Henry I.

1101 Robert of Normandy invades England because he thinks that, as William I's eldest son, he has more right to it than Henry, William's third son.

1106 Henry I defeats Robert and becomes Duke of Normandy.

The seal of King Henry II which would be used to make an image of the King on official documents.

1128 Henry I's daughter Matilda marries Geoffrey Plantagenet, Duke of Anjou (a large area of southwest France).

1135 Henry I dies. His nephew Stephen, the son of Henry's sister, becomes king. Matilda fights Stephen for the crown.

1144 Geoffrey of Anjou takes Normandy.

1150 Geoffrey of Anjou makes his and Matilda's son Henry duke of Normandy.

1153 King Stephen's son dies. Stephen agrees to let Henry of Anjou rule England after him.

1154 Stephen dies. Henry of Anjou becomes Henry II, the first non-Norman king of England since 1066.

1194 Norman rule ends in Italy.

1203–1204 The French king Philip Augustus conquers Anjou and Normandy.

The Feudal System

This was the social system that the Norman king William I introduced to England. He had taken most of the land away from the Anglo-Saxon (English) landowners, replacing them with Norman barons. Each major landowner needed a body of fighting men to protect his land, and the king wanted to be sure he would get military support when he needed it. So each baron made a promise to the king: in return for the king granting him his power and rank, the baron would provide men to make up a national army in time of war.

Knights were then the core of European fighting forces, so the knights were the backbone of the feudal system. In exchange for being available for military service, they were granted their own land and the support of their 'lord' (the landowner). The knights promised to be loyal to their lord, as the lords did to the king. The act of kneeling to swear loyalty was called 'paying homage'.

Knights (who were called 'vassals' of their lord) let peasants, members of the lowest social class, live on their land and farm it. These peasants were not free to move elsewhere, and to them the knight was the 'lord of the manor'. In return for being allowed to grow their own food, the peasants had to give some of it to the lord, as well as work on the lord's fields.

A portrait of King John hunting stag. Peasants could be sentenced to death for taking deer from the royal forests.

The Domesday Book

In 1085 William I decided to make the first listing of all property and goods in England. 'Domesday' is from the Latin *domus,* meaning 'house' (like 'domestic'). County by county, land was measured and recorded. So was livestock. Not one pig was left out. William used these numbers to keep control of the country and impose taxes. No later king or queen has achieved anything like it.

Pages from the Domesday Book, one of the most detailed ever surveys of property in England. The survey was carried out in 1086.

Medieval Food and Farming

Farming

In Europe during the Middle Ages most people lived in small villages and worked on the land. These peasant farmers were called 'serfs' or 'villeins'. They did not own their land, but had to pay for the right to farm it by working for the lord of the manor. They also had to give up part of their harvest to the lord. In some ways they were like slaves because they were not allowed to leave their village, get married, or even sell things without the lord's permission. With these rules it was nearly impossible for them to change their way of life.

This illustration from a 13th-century French Psalm book shows a peasant leading his pigs to graze. Noblemen often allowed peasants to bring pigs to their forests to feed on roots and nuts.

Instead of having all their land in one piece, serfs usually had strips of land spaced out on each of three big fields. One strip might have wheat growing on it, one might have barley, and the other might lie fallow (have no crops) to give the soil a rest. Serfs could also cut hay on meadows nearby and graze their cows, sheep, and goats in a common field. If they kept pigs they might be allowed to let them root around for nuts and roots in a forest on the lord's land.

Fast Food?

In the Middle Ages the church had some strict rules about not eating certain foods at special times. This was called fasting. Until around 1200 'four-footed flesh meat' was banned three days a week and on other fast days, such as Lent. On these days, people could have fish, such as salt herring. However, rich people were able to bend the rules. They had a much more varied diet than the poor, with fresh and imported foods, and could find more interesting substitutes for the forbidden meat. For example, someone decided that since beavers can swim, they could be counted as fish!

Food

Women from poor families would tend a vegetable garden at the back of the cottage, growing cabbages, onions, and herbs. They would have their grain ground at the mill, then

The Plough

By the year 1000 most people used a plough to turn the soil in their fields before planting their grain. A plough needed between four and eight oxen to pull it, because it was very heavy and hard to drag through the ground. Ordinary people could not afford both the plough and all those oxen on their own, so they depended on other families to team up with them, each sharing what they had.

they would make a heavy, coarse bread and take it to the village oven for baking. This was their most important food, along with porridge and pottage (thick soup). Water was not very safe to drink, because it might be contaminated, so most people drank ale made from fermented barley, even for breakfast!

Usually there was not enough hay to keep animals alive during the winter. People would kill some of their animals in the autumn, and smoke or salt the meat so it would keep longer. By the end of the winter, food might be very hard to come by, but wealthier people could often find game by hunting.

At mealtimes, stale bread or flat pieces of wood

These 12th-century German illustrations show how women often took on the job of harvesting and collecting grain. Part of the harvest would be given to the nobleman who owned the land.

called trenchers were used as plates, and people used their fingers to eat. If the food was soupy, a few people would share a bowl between them.

In the manor house, each meal might have many courses, served by waiters. The lord would take a pinch of salt from his special salt cellar as a signal for the meal to start, after a servant had tasted the food to check that it was not poisoned! After a feast leftover food was taken out to the gate where beggars and poor workers would be waiting.

Castles

The First Castles

In the early Middle Ages kings and lords began to live in castles for protection against their enemies. In the 10th century people began to build 'motte and bailey' castles. The motte was a mound of earth, on which a wooden or stone tower, or keep, was built, and this was surrounded by the bailey, a walled courtyard.

As the years went by castles began to get bigger and more comfortable. In early castles, everyone lived in the keep. As castles developed, they became like small towns. Inside the outer wall of large castles were huts to shelter villagers in times of war, servants' quarters, exercise yards, stables, a well, a bakery, gardens, and often a church.

Developments in Defence

Castles also began to get stronger and more resistant to enemy attack. Walls surrounding the castles added some protection. They were made with narrow slits to shoot arrows out of. The outside walls were protected by towers, which enabled soldiers to mount quick attacks on invaders. A drawbridge at the main entrance could be raised when an enemy approached. Finally, a deep moat around the castle made access even more difficult.

Enemies had to come up with all kinds of ways, and use them all at once, to attack a strong castle. They wheeled wooden towers up to the walls and tried to climb over the top. Catapults hurled stones and soldiers drove battering rams (long wooden beams with metal tips) at the walls to distract and confuse the people inside and to try and create a hole or crack. At the same time, archers bombarded the castle with arrows to try to drive the defenders back from the wall, while other attackers climbed ladders up the outer walls.

Parts of a Castle	
bailey	a walled courtyard
barbican	a tower at the gateway of a castle
battlements	a low wall around the top of a castle with slits to shoot arrows or guns through
curtain wall	the outer wall of a castle
keep	a large, central tower: the main building of a castle
moat	a deep ditch filled with water surrounding a castle
motte	a mound of earth on which a castle was built

The keep of Dover castle on the south coast of England. This strong, thick-walled building was built by Henry II towards the end of the 12th century.

14

Dover Castle seen from the air. The inner and outer walls around the keep were added by King John and Henry III, making Dover Castle a strong, well-defended fortress.

The development of gunpowder and firearms in the 14th century gave attackers the ability to destroy a castle easily. The age of the castle had ended.

British Castles

These are just a few of the medieval British castles that are still standing.

Century Built

11th	Edinburgh Castle, Scotland
11th	The Tower of London, England
12th	Dover Castle, England
12th	Rochester Castle, England
12th	Windsor Castle, England
13th	Arundel Castle, England
13th	Hever Castle, England
13th	Caernarfon Castle, Wales
14th	Beaumaris Castle, Wales
14th	Warwick Castle, England

Life in a Castle

Early castles were cold and dark. There was no glass in the windows, and the floors were made of stone. Waste from the toilets went straight into the moat. After a time the castle would become very smelly, and rich owners often went to one of their other castles when it got too bad. The owner of the castle had private living quarters and many servants. The owner's living rooms often had rush matting on the floors, and large fireplaces. Life was much less comfortable for the servants.

The remains of a garderobe (toilet) at Longtown Castle, near Hereford.

Every castle had a prison, which was usually a dark, damp, cramped room underground, which we now call a dungeon. Most prisoners were treated very badly. Sometimes they were tied to the walls with heavy chains, and often they were beaten and tortured. Special prisoners were treated better. They had lighter rooms and better food and were allowed to write letters and receive visitors. In England, the king's most important prisoners were sent to the Tower of London, from where it was almost impossible to escape.

Scotland, Wales, and Ireland

Edward I (ruled 1272–1307) wanted to be ruler of all of Britain, not just of England. Because he kept attacking Scotland, he got the nickname 'Hammer of the Scots'. He even stole the Stone of Destiny on which Scottish kings were crowned.

The Takeover of Wales

For centuries Wales had been ruled by its own princes. But from the time of the Norman conquest in the 11th century, the Anglo-Norman barons gradually took over Wales, beginning with the south. The northern land of Gwynedd held out, and its leader, Llywelyn, called himself the 'Prince of Wales'. He refused to give in to the English. In 1277 Edward surrounded Gwynedd with soldiers and ships, cutting off its food supply on the island of Anglesey. After hiding in the mountains of Snowdonia, the Welsh finally had to surrender.

Robert Bruce, who became King Robert I of Scotland, with his first wife, the Earl of Marr's daughter.

Five years later in 1282 Llywelyn and his brother started a rebellion, but they were killed, and their heads were put on spears in London to frighten people who might have similar ideas. Edward also built a ring of castles around Gwynedd to keep the Welsh in line.

In 1301 Edward called his own baby son the new Prince of Wales, and since then the heir to the British throne has been called by this name. Wales was never again under its own rule.

Scotland Wins Freedom

In 1291 there were a number of people claiming that they should be king of Scotland. Among them were Robert Bruce and John Balliol. Edward was asked to decide who should be king. He chose Balliol, who had to swear an oath of loyalty to Edward. In 1295 Balliol revolted against Edward, but in 1296 he was defeated and captured. The Scots, led by William Wallace, rose in rebellion against

Edward I of England, known as the Hammer of the Scots because of his frequent attacks on Scotland.

Edward. They were successful at first, but by 1303 the English were again in control. Wallace was captured, and in 1305 Edward had him hanged, drawn, and quartered. Pieces of Wallace's body were sent around Scotland as a warning to future rebels.

Robert Bruce, grandson of the Robert Bruce Edward had rejected, was crowned king of Scotland at Scone Palace in 1306. Edward led an army to Scotland but died on the way. Bruce went into hiding and fought a guerrilla war against the English. More and more Scots joined Bruce's cause, and in 1314 Edward II sent a vast army to Scotland. The Scots won a great victory over the English at Bannockburn. In 1320 the nobles of Scotland signed the Declaration of Arbroath, which said, 'As long as a hundred of us remain alive, we will not bow in any way to English dominion. For we fight, not for glory, riches, or honour, but for freedom alone'. Eventually, in 1328, the English recognized Scottish independence.

First Settlement of Ireland

Ireland was harder to get at than Scotland or Wales. It was cut off from mainland Britain by the sea, and split up into lots of different kingdoms, with warring rulers. Also, because it was poor, the English kings were not so tempted to conquer it. But in 1166 one of the Irish kings, Dermot MacMurrough, was banished from Ireland by the high king, Rory O'Connor. Some English lords agreed to help,

Carrickfergus Castle in Northern Ireland was built in 1180 by John de Courcy.

and one called Richard de Clare, or 'Strongbow', recaptured Leinster, and also the city of Dublin. He married Dermot's daughter and became king of Leinster when Dermot died. Later he and the other Irish kings vowed loyalty to King Henry II of England, making it possible for Henry to build English castles in Ireland for the first time. But the Irish resented the English settlers and it was the start of big problems between them.

Caernarfon Castle in Wales, built by Edward I in 1284, is one of Britain's most complex castles.

The Early Plantagenets

The first Norman kings, William I, William II, and Henry I, were harsh to the English, but strong rulers. However, Henry I's son had been drowned at sea and he had no male heir. Next in line to the throne was his daughter, Matilda, but some important people at court hated the idea of a woman ruler. They wanted Henry's nephew Stephen to be king instead, and quickly crowned him when Henry died in 1135. Matilda did not agree, so she and her French husband Geoffrey, Duke of Anjou, raised an army to fight Stephen. This war went on for 18 years, which made life hard for ordinary people.

Finally it was agreed that Matilda's son Henry would become king as Henry II. When Stephen died in 1154, Henry added England to all the land in France that he already owned. He was a stocky man with short red hair, and took charge of England by riding all over the countryside, together with about a hundred servants. He often surprised his hosts by arriving at very short notice! Henry pulled down or burned around 300 castles that had been built without royal permission, to show that he was in charge, and started up a professional army with the taxes he charged the barons.

The Yellow Flower

Henry II was known as Henry Plantagenet, from *plante genêt*, the French name of the yellow flower of the broom plant on the family crest. There is a legend that his father would wear a sprig of broom in his cap. Henry started a whole line of kings called the Plantagenets, which lasted for more than 300 years.

Eleanor of Aquitaine (about 1122–1204)

Eleanor of Aquitaine was the wife of Henry II. Before this, she had been married to the king of France and led her own troops in one of the crusades, dressed as an Amazon warrior! Because Henry was unfaithful to her, she encouraged her sons Richard and John, to start a rebellion. Henry then put Eleanor in prison for 15 years.

The first Plantagenet kings of England, Henry II, Richard I, John, and Henry III.

Richard was the third son of Henry II and twice fought against his father. He became King Richard I of England in 1189. He also ruled part of France, and hardly spent any time in England, so he may not even have spoken English. As soon as he became king, he went off on a crusade and had many adventures trying to capture Jerusalem. Because of his fearlessness, he was called the Lionheart.

While Richard was in the Holy Land, he insulted Duke Leopold of Austria. Later, because of a shipwreck on his way back home, he had to travel through Austria. Even though he was in disguise, Leopold captured him and put him in prison until the English had raised a huge ransom for their king to be set free.

The capture of Richard the Lionheart by Leopold of Austria is shown in this 12th-century book.

A 13th-century illustration showing the murder of Thomas à Becket by Henry II's knights in Canterbury cathedral.

Murder in the Cathedral

Thomas à Becket was a good friend and advisor of Henry II so when Henry made him archbishop of Canterbury, the top churchman in England, in 1162, he thought the church would go along with his ideas. But Thomas à Becket opposed some of Henry's new rules, saying they were against God's law.

One day Henry was fuming about Becket and said in front of his knights, 'Who will rid me of this turbulent priest?' Four knights took him seriously and rode straight to Canterbury to kill Becket. When they got there, the monks hurried Becket into the cathedral, thinking that the knights would respect such a holy place. Instead, they killed him in front of the altar.

This bloody murder shocked almost everyone, including Henry. The Pope made Becket a saint only three years later, and many people made pilgrimages to his tomb. Henry showed that he was sorry by walking barefoot through the streets of Canterbury, and getting the monks to whip him.

The Magna Carta

King John

When King Richard I of England died on 6 April 1199, he left behind him a country that was very hard to rule. Richard was a successful soldier who had earned the name 'Richard the Lionheart'. Although he had spent many years away from England fighting in the crusades, his people loved him. He was succeeded by his brother, John, who turned out to be very different.

King John was the youngest son of Henry II, and he was chosen as the next king by Richard himself. John inherited both the English throne and his family's lands in France. It was the loss of most of these French lands by 1204 that first made John unpopular with his people. He became more unpopular when he raised taxes to pay for the wars to win these lands back. John also argued with the church and in 1208 the Pope banned all church services in England, including baptisms and funerals. Eventually John received the most serious punishment the church could give - he was excommunicated, or cast out of the church. John resolved his problems with the church in 1213 by accepting Stephen Langton as Archbishop of Canterbury and paying an annual fee to the church.

John's problems with the barons grew, however. The failure of an expedition against the king of France in 1214 brought anger and resentment from the barons. Revolt began in the north and soon spread. The rebel barons captured London in May 1215. Stephen Langton intervened and managed to persuade the barons and John to meet to sort things out.

The seal of King John, used to show his agreement to the Magna Carta.

An effigy of King John at Worcester Cathedral, where he is buried.

King John (ruled 1199–1216): A Man of His Time

King John did accomplish some good things. It was King John who finished the first stone bridge over the River Thames in London. His father had begun the project but it was John who brought a French engineer to complete it. This marvellous bridge, which had 140 shops and 2 rows of houses on it, was opened in 1206 and lasted until it was knocked down and replaced 600 years later.

Although he had a reputation for working hard, King John also enjoyed himself. He loved hunting and holding banquets. He also loved taking a bath, which was extremely unusual at that time and thought to be very unhealthy.

The year 1216 was a bad one for John. While fleeing from the barons across the Wash, a broad river estuary to the north of East Anglia, John's heavy baggage carts, carrying all his war chests of money and jewels, got bogged down in quicksand and sank. He never saw them again. Later that year, on 18 October, John died at Newark Castle of dysentery, although the popular story says he died as a result of eating too many lampreys (a kind of fish) and peaches and drinking too much cider. He is buried in Worcester Cathedral.

Part of the Magna Carta, or Great Charter, one of the great documents of British history. It brought the monarchy under the rule of law for the first time.

Magna Carta

The document that became known as the Magna Carta, or Great Charter, is seen as a milestone in English history. The importance of Magna Carta is that it was the first time that it was made clear that there were laws that even the king must obey. It also granted, for the first time, rights and liberties to 'all freemen of the realm and their heirs for ever'.

In the weeks leading up to the signing of Magna Carta there were difficult discussions between the King and the barons, led by the archbishop of Canterbury. Eventually, John agreed to meet the barons in a field at Runnymede, on the banks of the River Thames between Staines and Windsor. After a short

ceremony on 15 June 1215, the royal seal was attached to the charter and copies were made and sent around the kingdom. However, shortly afterwards civil war broke out between John and the barons, and continued until John's death.

The original Magna Carta had 63 clauses and was written in Latin. Its most important points were that it limited the king's right to tax the barons and introduced the idea that no free man could be imprisoned unless he had been found guilty after a fair trial. The charter also said that the barons and the church had the right to remain free if they followed the laws of the land. The Magna Carta was rewritten in 1225 to keep it up to date.

The European Church in the Middle Ages

In medieval times everybody in the Christian countries of Western Europe belonged to the Roman Catholic Church. People did not really have a choice about what faith to belong to, and few questioned the teachings of the church. Religion was a very important part of people's lives, and ideas of heaven and hell were very real. Most people would have seen members of their own family die at a young age, so they had good reason to wonder about life after death.

The church was at the centre of village life. Everyone went to church to worship on Sundays. They were baptised and married there, and when they died they were buried there. Weddings usually took place at the church gates. The Roman Catholic Church also celebrated many feasts, saints' days, and other special occasions. Unfortunately, most people could not understand the words spoken in the Mass (service) by the priest, because they were all in Latin, and spoken behind a screen.

Shrines and Strange Relics

Many churches and cathedrals had shrines dedicated to a particular saint (holy man or woman). These were places for worship, and usually contained relics of the dead saint – pieces of bone, locks of hair, teeth, blood, or something the saint had touched. The more relics there were at the shrine, the more important it was for pilgrims to visit. People would leave a gift of money or gold at the shrine. They also usually needed somewhere to stay, and would buy souvenirs, such as badges, both of which raised money for the church or the local townspeople.

Relics were not just kept in church shrines. Everyone wanted a little holy treasure, which was thought to have supernatural powers. Pilgrims would carry tiny bits of relics in lockets and badges. Knights even hid them in the hilts of their swords. It is impossible that all of these relics were genuine, because there were so many of them. Some of the least believable relics that were bought and sold included drops of the Virgin Mary's milk, chips off the tablets of the Ten Commandments, and splinters of Jesus' cradle.

Ornate reliquaries like this were used to carry holy relics, objects associated with the saints. This one shows the death of Thomas à Becket.

22

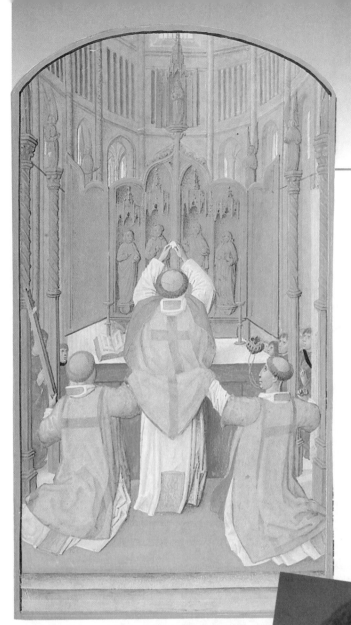

A Catholic priest is shown conducting a Mass.

The Priest

Most villages had a parish priest to say Mass and explain the faith to the ordinary people. Sometimes the priest would be the only person in the village who could read and write (although not always very well!), so he would have many duties, including writing down all the births, weddings, and deaths that happened through the year. He would also visit poor people, and give away food and clothing. Priests were not supposed to marry, although some did.

It was law that everyone should pay a tithe (one-tenth) of what they earned to the church. Peasant farmers would give a tenth of their crops to the church. The priest was also allowed to use church land to grow his own crops.

The shell worn by this pilgrim is associated with St James the Apostle.

Pilgrimage

In the Middle Ages going on pilgrimage (a journey to a holy place) was a popular thing to do. The top two places to visit were either Jerusalem in the Middle East, or Rome, where the pope lived, but most ordinary people couldn't go that far. They would travel instead to a holy shrine in their own country.

People believed that at a holy place their prayers would be answered more quickly, so it was a good place to ask for miraculous healing of an illness or another special favour. Also, to go on pilgrimage showed that people loved God and wanted to be holy themselves. Perhaps they wanted to show that they were sorry for their sins. Another reason was to thank God for an answered prayer.

Pilgrims usually travelled in groups, for safety and company. They would wear special clothes to show that they were on a holy journey, which might make robbers less likely to attack. As pilgrims walked together, they would tell stories, sing, and even play instruments to entertain themselves.

Popes and Emperors

Kings ruled their own countries, but in Western Europe there was one person higher than everyone: the pope. The pope was the head of the Roman Catholic Church, and nearly everybody belonged to this church. Because Catholics believed that the pope was God's representative on Earth, the pope was very powerful. Often the power of the Church competed with the power of kings and princes. The pope ruled over the archbishops, bishops, and priests in all the Catholic countries, and through them he could control the ordinary people, who feared that they would go to hell if they disobeyed the Church's teachings.

The Church owned a huge amount of land and money. Because people wanted to do good deeds to get into heaven, they gave money and valuable things to the Church, which made it even richer. The pope lived in Rome in a splendid palace.

Some people thought the Church was dishonest. Even though the pope and bishops were supposed to be especially holy, some of them cared more about power and a life of luxury. Top jobs in the church could be bought

Holy Father

The word pope comes from the Latin word for father, just as some children say 'Papa'. The pope is meant to be every Catholic's spiritual father. Popes would choose a special new name such as 'Innocent' or 'Leo' as soon as they became pope.

Pope Innocent III (ruled 1198–1216)

Pope Innocent III was a very powerful pope. He held a great council in 1215 and announced that popes had all the authority of God, and could tell rulers of Catholic countries what to do. He made Jews live apart from other people in ghettos and wear special badges to show that they were different.

Medieval people believed that their actions would be weighed up after their deaths, deciding whether they went to heaven or hell.

with money, or might be given to friends or relatives of the pope or the king. Also, the pope taught that people would spend many years in a terrible place called purgatory after they died, and the only way out was for people to buy 'indulgences', a way of paying for your sins. People who disagreed with the church's teachings were severely punished.

Holy Roman Empire

In the 9th century Charlemagne, the king of the Franks, was given a special title by the pope: emperor of Rome. He was to found a new Christian empire with all the glory of ancient Rome. If church and government combined their resources, they had the strength to gather great armies and the money to go on crusades. By the 13th century the emperors of Rome – most of whom were German – were calling themselves Holy Roman emperors. Popes thought that the Holy Roman emperors would help them rule countries, but often the emperors disagreed with the popes and even fought wars against them. They argued about many things, but particularly about whether

Frederick I was an outstanding leader. He was the first to add the word Holy to the title of Roman emperor.

Frederick I was a German emperor with the nickname Barbarossa, which means 'red beard'. He was thought to be one of the greatest of the Holy Roman emperors. He had his hands full, trying to control the countries that he ruled, and fighting with the pope. Once, just as he was invading Rome, his army was overcome by a terrible plague. In 1189 Barbarossa set off on a crusade, but drowned in a river before he even got to the Holy Land.

popes should pick who would be emperor, or whether emperors should pick who would be pope.

In 1075 Emperor Henry IV and Pope Gregory VII had a big argument. Henry tried to remove Gregory, and Gregory excommunicated Henry (expelled him from the church). Henry lost the support of his nobles, and two years later he was forced to go to Canossa in northern Italy to beg the Pope to forgive him. Gregory did so, but only after he made him wait for two days in a snowstorm!

Frederick II (ruled 1220–1250)

Frederick II was Holy Roman emperor like his grandfather Barbarossa, and was called 'The Wonder of the World' because he was so mighty. He was interested in learning and started the University of Naples and a medical school. He also spoke many languages and wrote poetry in Italian. He organized a crusade that was delayed for five years, but when he finally went, his army captured Bethlehem and Nazareth. After making a deal with the Muslims, Frederick crowned himself king of Jerusalem.

A representation of Frederick II added to the tomb of the Charlemagne, king of the Franks.

25

Monks and Monasteries

In the Middle Ages many people felt that the best way of serving God was to become a monk. To do this, they would take religious vows, promising to live in a special place called a monastery, and to spend their time praying, working, and obeying the monastery rules. The first rules had been set out by St Benedict in the 6th century, and the monks that followed his rules were called Benedictines. Monks could not get married or have children. They were not allowed to keep anything of their own, and had to live a poor and simple life. To show that they had become separate from the world, their hair was tonsured (shaved off at the top) and they wore special robes.

St Francis with some of his followers. The bird above his head represents the Holy Spirit.

Life in the Monastery

Monasteries, also called abbeys and priories, were communities of people, living together for life. The head of a monastery was called an abbot or a prior. The monks had to pray eight set times a day, beginning at 2 a.m., and couldn't miss any of the chapel services unless they were ill.

Usually monks worked at different jobs such as farming or making things, and some monasteries became famous for the quality of their goods. Some monks looked after poor or sick people in the local villages. Other monks were scholars, studying or copying old manuscripts (hand-written books). The books would be decorated with tiny pictures called illuminations. Some monks wrote their own books about what they had seen or discovered.

A monastery was like a small village, with its own hospital, fields for growing food, workshops, kitchens, dining rooms, a cloister (covered walkway), sometimes a school, and rooms for travellers. Often the toilets and plumbing were more advanced in monasteries than they were elsewhere. In the centre of the monastery was the church, sometimes a fine cathedral. In some places the monasteries became very rich, and owned large areas of land. Sometimes the monks in such monasteries began to live lives of luxury. To avoid this, new orders of monks, the Cistercians and Carthusians, were founded, and these new orders followed much harsher rules.

These 14th-century illustrations show scenes from the daily lives of students training to be monks.

A 13th-century illustration of St Francis surrounded by scenes from Bible stories.

Nuns and Nunneries

Women also took up the monastic life. They were called nuns, but there were not as many nuns as monks. They lived in convents (sometimes also called nunneries). Like monks, they often looked after travellers, or ran hospitals. This was one of the few kinds of healthcare available to people in the Middle Ages. There were also schools in convents, which were often very strict. The head of the convent was called the abbess.

St Francis (about 1182–1226)

Francis was the son of a rich man in Assisi, Italy. He gave away all he owned, even his clothes, out of love for Jesus Christ. His father was very angry, but Francis started a religious group, called friars, or 'little brothers'. They did not live in monasteries, but walked around the country teaching people about God. Francis was famous for his love for all creatures, and there are many stories about how even wild animals became tame when he talked to them. The many people who followed Francis were called Franciscans, and his friend Clare, a beautiful noblewoman, started her own order called the Poor Clares in 1212.

Monks' Meals

In the earlier part of the Middle Ages the food eaten by monks and nuns was very plain indeed. Although they had to get up in the night for prayer, they might not get any breakfast. There was a main meal at noon with no meat, and just a small supper before the sun set, with no snacks in between. During the meals, one of the nuns or monks would read out loud from a religious book. No one else was allowed to talk, and they would have to use hand signals to show what they wanted!

Most monasteries would give food or lodging to anyone who came to the door, and they would serve their best meals for visitors. There was usually honey from the beehives that were kept for making candle wax, and other dainty foods for special occasions. As the years went by, many religious orders started to be less strict and served better food, especially if they had become rich and prosperous. Monasteries were often famous for their wine or mead (an alcoholic drink made from honey).

Churches, Cathedrals, and Universities

Gothic Architecture

Gothic architecture was a style of building that began in the mid-12th century and lasted for about 350 years. It was used mostly for churches – including many vast and magnificent cathedrals. Buildings changed considerably with this new style of architecture. They became taller, with high ceilings and tall spires. One of the main features of Gothic architecture is the pointed arches, often used for windows.

Before the 12th century, heavy stone vaults, which were used to hold the ceiling up, often put so much pressure on the walls that they pushed the walls outwards. This would sometimes make the buildings collapse. Gothic buildings were stronger and more stable than many previous buildings because of their new system of rib vaulting and flying buttresses. In the early 12th century architects invented a new type of vault, the ribbed vault, that was thinner and lighter. They designed buildings with ribbed vaults running horizontally, vertically, and diagonally. This system of vaults was stable without being too heavy. Flying buttresses were arches on the outside of the building that supported the vaults. This system enabled architects to design stronger buildings with thinner walls, higher ceilings, and huge glass windows.

Why is it called Gothic?

The word 'Gothic' was first used by architects much later, during the Renaissance. They were very critical of the architecture of the Middle Ages, favouring the older classical architecture.

Part of the west front of Wells Cathedral, Somerset, which has more than 300 life-size statues. Work on the cathedral began in 1175.

Famous Gothic Churches

Date Begun	Church	Country
1160	Notre-Dame de Paris	France
1174	Canterbury Cathedral	England
1194	Chartres Cathedral	France
1220	Salisbury Cathedral	England
1245	Westminster Abbey	England
1248	Cologne Cathedral	Germany
1261	York Minster	England
1386	Milan Cathedral	Italy

An Italian architect and painter called Giorgio Vasari may have made up the term when he blamed the style on the Goths, a barbarian people who had destroyed the Roman Empire and its classical architecture in the 5th century.

The University of Bologna

The oldest university in the world that is still open today is the University of Bologna, in Italy.

One of the many gargoyles that decorate the cathedral of Notre-Dame in Paris.

It started out as a school of law in the 11th century and became a fully established university in the early 14th century. It became very famous during the Middle Ages. The Italian poets Dante and Petrarch were two of its students.

Oxford University

Oxford is the oldest university in the English-speaking world, and many of its colleges are fine examples of Gothic architecture. It was an important centre of learning as early as the 12th century, when scholars from Europe settled there. In the mid-13th century members of Christian religious orders such as the Dominicans and Franciscans settled in Oxford and formed small communities committed to education. Wealthy individuals also created small communities by giving money to establish them. These communities turned into colleges. One of the earliest colleges is called Balliol. It was named after the king of Scotland, John Balliol, because his parents gave the money to start it.

Cambridge University

Cambridge is the second oldest university in Britain. It started up in a similar way to Oxford, with religious orders establishing

Gargoyles

Gargoyles had a practical purpose. They were spouts that projected out from gutters to take rainwater away from the outside walls. In Gothic architecture they were made of stone and often carved into frightening-looking imaginary animals, angels, and human heads.

A 14th-century Italian sculpture showing students with their teacher. The world's oldest university is in Italy.

Westminster Abbey

Westminster Abbey in London is the most visited church in Britain. Its official name is the Collegiate Church of St Peter in Westminster, and it stands 31 metres (102 feet) tall. King Edward the Confessor began building it in 1050, but it was rebuilt in the Gothic style beginning in 1245. Most English kings and queens, starting with William the Conqueror in 1066, have been crowned in the abbey. Many of them are also buried there, along with many famous English people, including the scientist Sir Isaac Newton and the poet Geoffrey Chaucer.

houses of residence (places to stay). In the early 13th century some students left Oxford and went to study at Cambridge. Hugh de Balsham, bishop of Ely, founded Peterhouse, the first college at Cambridge, in 1284. Cambridge was officially recognized as a university by Pope John XXII in 1318.

Medieval Warfare

The Military System

Kings and noblemen ruled their lands from castles built in easily defended places, such as a hill above a valley where there was an important road or river. They relied on mounted knights and foot soldiers to help them keep their power, to defend their castles, and to attack the castles of their enemies. Knights came largely from the upper classes. Until around the 14th century lords recruited their foot soldiers from peasants, labourers, workers, and even criminals. At the beginning of the 14th century, they began to hire mercenaries (foreign soldiers who would work for anyone who paid them). Sometimes the nobles would pay a sum of money to the king to hire an army rather than providing soldiers themselves.

Sieges

A siege was a way to weaken or destroy a castle. An attacking army would surround the castle, camping a safe distance away. By preventing anyone inside from getting any food or other supplies, they would eventually force the people inside to come out and surrender.

A 14th-century German illustration showing King John I of Brabant leading his knights into battle.

A Successful Siege: Bedford Castle

Bedford Castle in England was owned by a Frenchman, Falkes de Bréauté, who was a friend of King John. After the death of the king in 1216, the English barons wanted the French soldiers out. One of these barons, Hubert de Burgh, marched with an army to take over Bedford Castle in 1221.

Hubert began his attack by bringing up two wooden towers to the outer wall of the castle. His archers were then able to shoot arrows over the wall killing many of the defenders. Next he brought up battering rams (long wooden beams with metal tips) and other siege machines to make a breach (hole) in the wall. Once inside his engineers dug a mine under the walls of the keep (central building) and set fire to the wooden props in the tunnel, causing a corner of the keep to sink lower in the ground and the wall to tear. After that the French soldiers surrendered and begged for mercy. Hubert hanged some of them, sent the others back to France, and completely destroyed the castle.

This 14th-century illustration shows how both men and women joined in helping to defend a castle from attack.

Some examples of swords and a scabbard from the Middle Ages. These were made in Spain.

Sometimes the soldiers inside the castle would outsmart the attackers by sneaking out through a secret gate, called a salleyport, at the back of a castle. Under the cover of night they would make a surprise attack on the enemy camp.

Armour

Chain mail was common from the 6th century to the 13th century. Made of interlocking wire rings, it was relatively light and comfortable and allowed the soldier to move around, but it didn't protect against heavy maces (spiked clubs) and axes.

As weapons became more advanced, armour had to become stronger. In the 13th century armour specialists developed plate armour for both knights and horses. At first knights wore four pieces to cover just their knees and elbows. Soon these pieces extended to cover their entire arms and legs. During the next century armour developed more and more. By the 15th century armour would encase a knight from head to toe. Special bolts and straps allowed the body to move, and the helmet had a moveable visor protecting the face. Shields became less important because plate armour was so strong. However, it was a lot heavier and less flexible than chain mail.

The invention of guns made armour impractical. If it was thick enough to stop a bullet, it would be too heavy to wear. By the 16th century a knight was no longer a warrior.

Medieval Weapons

crossbow	a powerful bow fastened to a wooden support, usually rested on the shoulder. The arrow is held and then released by pulling a trigger.
longbow	a long wooden bow with a greater rate of fire than a crossbow
spear	a sharp metal point on a long pole, either thrown or used to stab
pike	a type of long spear used by foot soldiers
lance	a long spear carried by a horseman
mace	a large, heavy club usually having a head with metal spikes
battleaxe	a heavy blade (sometimes two blades) on a long wooden handle
dagger	a short, pointed knife used for stabbing
sword	a long, handled blade used for hacking and stabbing
sling	a loop used for hurling stones
catapult	a siege machine for hurling spears and stones
ballista	a siege machine for throwing heavy stones up to 45 kg/100 lbs
trebuchet	a giant sling used in sieges

Knights and Chivalry

The Feudal System

Medieval European kings spent much of their time defending their kingdoms while at the same time trying to conquer new lands. In order to do this, they had to have a system that kept soldiers loyal to them. This was the feudal system. The kings gave the knights who served them portions of land as gifts, and in turn these knights let out portions of this land to peasant farmers who in return had to fight when needed in battles. This arrangement guaranteed the king an army immediately when he needed it, because his followers had to serve him in order to keep their land. This way of raising an army lasted in Europe until around the 13th century. After that, soldiers were usually paid professionals.

A 14th-century illustration showing the arrival of a knight at a castle.

Armour and Heraldry

Knights wore armour from head to toe to protect them from swords and spears. At first they wore chain mail, made from interlocking wire rings, over thick leather. Later they wore plate armour which protected them better, but which was very heavy, weighing up to 30 kilograms (66 pounds)!

Because there was no way to identify knights under their armour, each knight chose his own special symbol, called his 'arms'. He wore this symbol sewn onto a tunic over his armour, and this was his 'coat of arms'. Particular symbols became identified with particular families. These coats of arms were kept as family badges and were passed down through the generations of a family. Heraldry is the study of the coats of arms.

Knights and Chivalry

Knights were soldiers who rode on horseback and wore armour. At first, any boy could become a knight, but soon only rich families could afford horses and armour for their sons. Since kings relied on the loyalty of knights to help protect them and get new lands, a strict code of behaviour for knights developed. This code is now called chivalry. It was based on honour, loyalty, bravery, courtesy, and obedience. A knight was expected to be a brave soldier as well as gentle. He should be strong, manly, and ruthless, but also polite, cultured, and religious. A lot of stories from this time, such as the legends of King Arthur, were based on knights and chivalry, but in real life few knights lived up to this code of conduct, particularly when dealing with people from lower classes.

The Education of a Knight

Knighthood was considered a great honour, and boys were trained for it starting from the age of seven. Even kings had to train for knighthood. First the boys served as pages in the household of the king or lord who employed their father. During this time they learned about the rules of knighthood and how to use weapons. Next, when the boys were about 15, they worked as servants to knights and were known as squires. During this time they learned how to fight on horseback and all the other skills they needed to become knights.

Two knights compete in a tournament. Their coats of arms can be seen decorating their horses' coverings.

After about five years, if successful, a squire would become a knight. Before the official ceremony he would stay up all night in a chapel, thinking about the responsibilities and privileges of his new life. Then he would be dubbed, or touched on the shoulders with a sword, and presented with a set of golden spurs, which were one of the symbols of knighthood.

Nowadays English queens and kings still knight people, but they do this only as a symbolic award of honour.

Knights battle fiercely in a tournament in this 14th-century illustration.

Tournaments and Jousting

Tournaments took place during peacetime as competitions between knights. During the 11th century large groups of knights participated in mock battles. By the 13th century knights began participating in one-to-one tournaments. They jousted on horseback (charged at each other with lances), or fought using weapons with long wooden handles and metal heads to knock their opponents to the ground. Knights were often injured during jousting competitions.

Knights also participated in medieval duels, which were any type of one-to-one fight used to settle disputes. A knight would throw down his glove or hat and demand a duel with someone who had insulted his honour.

The Development of Language

Parlez-vous Anglais?

Before 1066 most people in England spoke Anglo-Saxon or Old English. When the Normans took over England they brought their own language, Norman-French. Everyone in authority had to spread French, the language of the new rulers of England. English was the language of the common people. Eventually English became the official language again in 1362, but by that time a great many French words had become part of everyday speech.

Manuscripts, hand-written books, are carefully filed away by monks in this 14th-century illustration.

Old to Middle to Modern

Before the Normans came the people spoke a language we now call Old English. After the Normans came, Old English started to change so much that we call it Middle English, more like the English we speak now. Even so, both Old and Middle English would probably sound like foreign languages to us today. Here are some of the differences:

Old	Middle	Modern
mycel	muchel	much
fyr	fuir	fire
goda	gode	good
naefre	nevere	never

Many Old English words – like folk, baker, fisherman, shepherd, and weaver – have to do with ordinary people and the countryside. However, many of the French words that became a part of the English language had to do with things that the Normans controlled. Lance, battle, and castle are Norman words that showed their power in war. Mayor, crime, judge, and prisoner are Norman words that were used as they were ruling the country. Some other words that came into English show the French love of food, like pork, beef, sauce, dinner, and feast. We are so used to these borrowed words that they don't seem foreign to us any more.

Layers of Language

When the Romans arrived in Britain in the 1st century AD all the people who lived there spoke Celtic languages – the ancestors of modern Gaelic and Welsh. These Celtic languages still survive in some English place names, such as Avon as a name for several rivers. The Romans, who spoke Latin, left their stamp on many place names. The Latin word for camp, *castra,* is in place names like Chester and Winchester, which shows us how old those cities are. From the 5th century peoples called Angles, Jutes, and Saxons came from Denmark and Germany to settle in England. They brought their own Germanic languages, which became Anglo-Saxon, or what we usually call Old English. That is why many old words such as father, mother, bread, and butter, are almost the same in German as they are in English.

The Anglo-Saxon settlers pushed the Celtic-speaking peoples to the north and west, and today Celtic languages are spoken only in parts of Scotland, Ireland, and Wales. Hardly any Celtic words came into English. A few are bog, whisky, and basket. Around AD 600, though, Roman missionaries brought Latin back to England. Lots of Latin words came into the English language, for example, priest, nun, and monk. The Vikings from Scandinavia who invaded the north and east of England between the 9th and the 11th centuries gave us almost all English words beginning with 'sk', such as skin, skill, sky, and skirt, from their Norse languages.

The first page of Beowulf, an epic poem most likely written in the 8th century, telling the story of the hero Beowulf.

An illustration from a 14th-century Italian manuscript. A woman is shown hearing the news of her husband's death.

Learning Latin

For many years Latin was the language used by educated people all over Europe for speaking and writing. Most people in the Middle Ages never learned to read and write at all. Instead, they often learned a trade or laboured in the fields. However, the children of richer families might be taught by nuns or priests, either in a cathedral or monastery, or a grammar school. Latin was almost the only subject that was taught, because it was thought to be the most important – the Bible was only written in Latin and church services were all in Latin.

Storytelling

In medieval times most people could not read or write, and few people could afford to buy books. There were no newspapers or telephones to bring news of the world, and no tapes, radio, or television to give information. Instead, storytellers passed

Marie de France (about 1150–1215)

Marie was a French poet who was born in France around the middle of the 12th century, but lived most of her life in England. She is the first known French or English woman writer. Her poems were written in a language called Anglo-Norman, an old mixture of French and English.

Troubadours travelled from town to town to play music and tell tales of bravery and love.

on history and legends by word of mouth. Women skilled in needlework would sew pictures of famous events. An example of this is the Bayeux Tapestry, a very long strip of cloth embroidered with pictures and words which tell the whole story of the Battle of Hastings.

Bands of wandering minstrels visited castles and marketplaces, singing sad and comic songs accompanied by a lute or bagpipes. In the south of France men called troubadours played instruments and sang poetic ballads about courtly love and the brave deeds of knights. Travelling entertainers such as minstrels, acrobats, and jugglers were especially popular, because they brought the latest pieces of news and gossip from other parts of the country for everyone to hear.

Mummers, Miracles, and Mysteries

Town guilds (groups of craftsmen) had pageants (shows) every year with plays based on a story from the Bible, or the life of a saint. Because a person's craft or trade was called their 'mystery' in those days, they were called mystery plays, or sometimes miracle plays. Each guild might have its own speciality

Doom Paintings

A medieval church could have been dull for peasants, because the priest said the Mass behind a screen in Latin, a language that ordinary people could not understand. However, the wood carvings, cloth hangings, statues, and murals along the walls of the church building told vivid stories in pictures of Bible characters and saints. Often there was a Doom Painting of the fearful Day of Judgement, showing sinners dropping into hell to be tortured by devils, and saved people being brought by angels up into heaven.

An illustration from the tale of King Arthur, the legendary king of England. The Arthur stories have been popular for close to a thousand years.

Illuminations

Books had to be hand-written at this time, usually by monks or nuns in a special room called a scriptorium. They could only do a few pages a day, writing with a quill pen. The pages were then decorated with tiny pictures called illuminations. Gold leaf (very thin gold) was pressed onto the designs.

Geoffrey of Monmouth and the Legends of King Arthur

Around 1135 a Welsh monk called Geoffrey of Monmouth wrote a book called the *History of the Kings of Britain*. It included the famous legends of King Arthur and his knights. In the story, elves give Arthur magical gifts and powers.

A German lord reads poetry. In the 14th century few people knew how to read or write.

subject, such as Adam and Eve, or Paradise. Usually each separate scene in the play would be acted on a different moving cart, so that crowds in the street could stand in one place and watch the whole story as it went by. Some plays lasted for days, telling the whole Christian story.

Wandering actors would also take plays to barons' castles or manor houses. Mime actors called mummers performed their plays – lively folk tales – during the Twelve Days of Christmas and other feast days and festivals. These mime plays were the beginning of modern-day pantomimes. Props, jokes, and special effects – like manure falling out of a donkey costume – added to the fun.

The Rise of Islam: Muhammad and the Five Pillars

By the beginning of the 11th century the religion of Islam, a word which means 'surrender' or 'submission', had existed for almost four centuries. Islam and its followers, called Muslims, had increased in number as the teachings of one man, Muhammad, spread from Arabia into North Africa, Asia, and southern Europe.

Muhammad was born in Mecca in Arabia about AD 570. At that time Arabs worshipped more than one god, which made them very different from Jews and Christians who worshipped only one god.

Muhammad's Experience

When Muhammad was about 40 years old, he had an encounter with an angel who told him

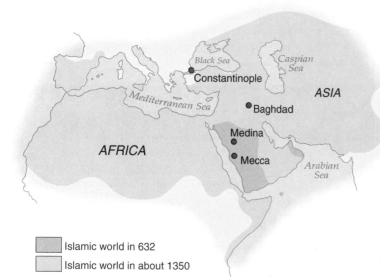

Black Sea
Caspian Sea
Constantinople
Mediterranean Sea
ASIA
Baghdad
Medina
AFRICA
Mecca
Arabian Sea

Islamic world in 632
Islamic world in about 1350

Muslim Science

In the Middle Ages Muslim countries were far ahead of Christian Europe in certain subjects such as mathematics, astronomy, and medicine. Muslim scholars translated and preserved much of the work of the ancient Greek philosophers and scientists, which had been lost in Christian Europe after the fall of the Roman Empire. They also produced more accurate observations of the stars than the Greeks had done. Borrowing from India, Arab mathematicians used a nought, or zero, and developed the way of writing numbers that we use today. The Arab mathematician al-Khwarizmi wrote an important book about algebra in the 9th century. The word 'algebra' itself comes from his name. Much of Arab learning in the fields of mathematics, medicine, and science was collected in a great encyclopedia by the Persian philosopher and physician Avicenna in the early 11th century.

A Muslim doctor is shown preparing an antidote to a poison in this 12th-century Arab book. According to Islamic belief 'God sends down no malady without also sending down with it a cure'.

This page from the Koran, the sacred book of the Muslim faith, was written in Persia (now Iran) in the 9th century.

that there was only one God. This was the first of many such visions, which Muslims believe were the direct words of God. Muhammad felt that he had been chosen by God, whom he called Allah, as a messenger, or prophet. He spent the rest of his life spreading God's word to the Arab people.

The Five Pillars of Islam

Muhammad as the the prophet of God taught that it was not enough just to follow a religion. It was also important to live a good life and for all followers to belong to a single community. Muhammad, the prophet, presented a set of rules for Muslims to live by. These rules, called the Five Pillars of Islam, were and still are strictly followed by all Muslims.

Muhammad had to flee from Mecca in AD 622 because the people there were against his teachings. But in his new home of Medina, another city in Arabia, his preaching was soon accepted and he returned to Mecca to establish a strong Islamic community and state. It was

after Muhammad's death in 632 that all of his revelations (visions) were gathered in one scripture called the Koran (or Qur'an).

With Muhammad gone, a series of caliphs, or successors, governed the Islamic state and a period of Islamic conquests and empire building began. The war outside Arabia against non-Muslims, whom Muslims called 'unbelievers', became known as a *jihad*, or holy war.

Five Pillars of Islam

Five duties, known as the Five Pillars of Islam, are very important to Muslims. The first duty requires all Muslims to publicly declare their faith by saying at least once, 'There is no God but Allah and Muhammad is his Prophet'. The second duty is to pray five times every day, at a mosque (a Muslim place of worship) if possible. The third duty requires a Muslim to pay a special tax to help the poor. The fourth duty is to fast (not eat or drink) between sunrise and sunset during a month-long period called Ramadan. The fifth duty is to make a pilgrimage to Mecca at least once in a lifetime if you are wealthy and healthy enough.

The Rise of Islam: Seljuks and Sufism

The Sultanhani Caravanserai was one of the stops along the Silk Road trading route through Asia.

By the 11th century the Muslim religion had expanded at a rate that alarmed the Christian world. The head of the Christians, the pope in Rome, began to fear the increasing strength of Islam. This period saw the beginning of a deep mistrust between the two religions.

The Seljuk Empire

A Turkish people called the Seljuks from Central Asia were converted to Islam in the 10th century. They moved eastwards towards the Arab countries early in the 11th century, where they began to build an empire. Their leader, Togrul Beg, conquered the city of Baghdad and most of the area that forms modern Iraq and Iran. Later, Togrul's successors, Alp Arslan and Malik Shah, moved into Syria and Anatolia (modern Turkey). They captured what Christians called the 'Holy Land' of Palestine and made war on the Christian city of Constantinople (modern Istanbul).

Alarmed by the Seljuks' invasion, in 1095 Pope Urban II called for a series of military campaigns called crusades to take back the Holy Land for Christianity. The crusaders succeeded in recapturing Jerusalem in 1099 and built castles to guard their conquests. Over the next 150 years Christians organized six more crusades against the Muslims, but most failed.

The interior of the mosque of Sultan Ahmed in Istanbul, Turkey. It is often called the Blue Mosque for the colour of the tiles used.

Islamic Architecture

Domes, minarets, arches, arcades, and courtyards are all distinctive features of Islamic architecture. The dome was originally developed from Roman and early Christian architecture. The Seljuks imitated the Iranian squinches (small arches at the corners of a square) often used to support smaller domes. This led to the spread of domed mosques and palaces throughout the Islamic world. These buildings were highly decorated. Images of prophets and saints are not allowed in Muslim buildings, so imaginative design was important. The Seljuks introduced glazed bricks and tiles. Mosaic, woodcarving, and Arabic calligraphy were other forms of architectural decoration.

The mosque is the centre of a Muslim's life. Prayers are said in the mosque five times a day while facing Mecca. As Mecca is the birthplace of the Muslim prophet Muhammad, the wall of the mosque closest to Mecca has a niche or hollow, called a *mihrab,* to show the direction of the city. Mecca is also the place where the Kaaba is found. A small square building, the Kaaba contains a black stone that is sacred to Muslims. They believe that it is the stone that was given to Adam when he was expelled from paradise. It now stands inside a huge mosque known as al-Haram, or Great Mosque.

The mihrab of the Great Mosque at Cordoba, Spain. The mihrab shows the direction of Mecca, the Muslim holy city and is often highly decorated.

Sufism

Meanwhile, the Muslim faith itself was undergoing a series of changes. The 12th century saw the increased acceptance of Sufism, a mystical (spiritual) form of Islam. Sufis aimed for a stronger religious experience in their daily lives. Sufi missionaries spread the Islamic faith to India, Central Asia, Turkey, and Africa.

Islam had moved far from its first period of growth. Muslim traders travelled widely, and by the 14th century had converted people to Islam in countries as far away as Indonesia, Malaya, and China. Islam was now a religion of all races and cultures, held together by a shared belief in the one God and the teachings of the prophet Muhammad.

Alp Arslan (ruled 1063–1072)

The Seljuk Turk leader Alp Arslan, whose name means 'courageous lion', was the nephew of Togrul Beg. His greatest enemies were the Fatimids, a powerful Muslim family who ruled Egypt, and the Christian Byzantine Empire. In 1071 Alp Arslan defeated the Byzantine army at the Battle of Manzikert and took the Byzantine emperor, Romanus IV, as prisoner. Although he later released the emperor, this great triumph made Alp Arslan very famous in Islamic history.

Song China

Chinese civilization is one of the oldest in the world, and by AD 1000 it had been ruled by dynasties (lines of emperors) for nearly 2,500 years. The Song dynasty was founded in 960 by the northern general Zhao Kuangyin, known as

Kaifeng

Hangchow

—— Song empire in 960

southern Song empire in 1127

Chin empire in 1127

Emperor Taizu. Together with his brother, he brought together the different parts of China to create the Chinese empire in 978. Medieval China under the Song was more advanced than Europe in many ways. Government, trade, industry, arts, and sciences all thrived during this time. The Song dynasty ruled until 1279, when China was conquered by the Mongols.

The Song dynasty is divided into two periods. During the Northern Song period (960–1126) the capital was at Kaifeng. When Northern China was invaded by the Liao kingdom, the Song went to the Chin people for help. The Chin helped the Song to defeat the Liao, but then the Chin turned on their allies and in 1126 invaded Northern Song China, taking the capital. During the Southern Song period

(1127–1279), when the Chin ruled Northern China, the Song emperors moved the capital south to the city of Hangchow.

Government

Over the previous 1,000 years the Chinese had developed an efficient and stable form of government run by civil servants (government workers). It was not the nobles or generals who advised the emperor and ruled the provinces, but the civil servants. Men could not become civil servants by bribery or by being related to powerful people. Instead, they had to study hard and pass a series of exams. The Song tightened up the rules about who could become a civil servant, made the exams more difficult, and established schools where poor but clever boys could study.

Economy

The Chinese were relatively prosperous during the Song dynasty. Cities grew quickly and were linked by trade. Kaifeng, for example, which was the capital of the Song empire, had a population in 1120 of over a quarter of a million, whereas London only had a population of a few thousand. By the 13th century several cities with a population of more than 1 million people flourished along rivers and the southeast coast. Farmers harvested rice, cotton, and tea, and workers and artisans produced fine porcelain and silk. Many of these products were exported, making the Chinese richer.

Neo-Confucianism

A new philosophy based on the ideals taught by the ancient Chinese philosopher Confucius became popular during the Song dynasty. It was established by a group led by the philosopher Zhu Xi in the 12th century. Neo-Confucians believed that everyone and everything is created in a certain way to work together to make the world a better place. They believed that all people are born good, and that they must work to become aware of the good qualities that they are born with. Society breaks down when people forget these good qualities and act selfishly. Zhu and his followers believed in helping people in need, and set up charities to help feed the hungry.

Arts

The government exams were based on literature, and so people who wanted to join the government spent years studying history, philosophy, and the classics. More people were able to read and write than ever before. Printing with movable type was invented, and books became very popular. Scholars were also interested in painting, pottery, poetry, music, calligraphy, and collecting works of art. Song architecture featured very tall buildings, especially pagodas, Buddhist temples with six or eight sides.

This beautifully carved jar shows how skilled the craftsworkers of Song China were.

This painting from the Song period shows a doctor at work. It must be a painful treatment as the patient is being held down!

Inventions and Technologies of Song China

Bank notes
Gunpowder
Magnetic compass
Movable type printing
Water clock
Multi-colour printing
Rocket
Bomb with shrapnel
Cannon
Sundial
Land mine

The Khmer Empire

The God-Kings

The Khmer empire was founded in 802 by the powerful young king Jayavarman II. His rule united the lands that are now Cambodia, Laos, Thailand, and Vietnam. The people believed that he, and his successors, were gods. Under

This intricately carved scene of warriors decorates one of the walls at the temple of Angkor Wat.

the god-kings, the Khmers grew wealthy. Rice grew well on the fertile banks of the Mekong River and Lake Tonle Sap. The Khmers developed a complex irrigation system that made it possible for them to harvest three crops a year. Between the 9th and 15th centuries the Khmer empire dominated Southeast Asia,

King Jayavarman VII (ruled 1181–about 1218)

The Khmer empire reached its peak during the reign of Jayavarman VII. He conquered Champa in modern Vietnam, and extended his rule to the Malay peninsula and part of Burma. He built stone walls and moats to protect Angkor from attack, and constructed roads, hospitals, and temples throughout the empire. He also built many monuments in Angkor and elsewhere, decorated with wall sculptures that celebrate his victories over the people of Champa.

capturing slaves, treasure, and land from the conquered nations.

The Golden Age of Angkor

King Yasovarman I moved the capital of Khmer from Roluos to Angkor in 889. This was the spiritual centre for the Khmers, and over 60 temples were built there. At its peak, the city had a population of about 1 million people, supported by palaces, hospitals, and a clever system of reservoirs and canals. Today many of the ruins of Angkor are covered up by the jungle of the rainforest, but the ruined temples and fascinating irrigation system that remain reveal that the Khmer people were highly skilled architects and engineers.

The Temple of Angkor Wat

The temple of Angkor Wat was built by King Suryvarman II between 1113 and 1150. It is the most beautiful and famous monument in Angkor, and is one of the largest religious structures ever built. The temple is dedicated to Vishnu, the Hindu god who preserves the universe. Lavish stone carvings decorate its walls and columns, telling sacred Hindu stories, depicting victorious Khmer battles, and showing scenes of everyday life. The longest continuous bas-relief (wall carving) in the world runs along the outer gallery walls.

Like all Hindu temples, Angkor Wat was designed to represent the universe. Four great gateways invite worshippers to pass from the realm of humans to the realm of the gods. The central tower, which was once covered in gold, rises 65 metres (210 feet) into the sky to link earth with heaven. It symbolizes Mount Meru, which Hindus believe is the centre of the universe.

44

The magnificent temple of Angkor Wat. For centuries it was lost in the jungle until its rediscovery by French explorers in the 18th century.

A carved stone scene showing an elephant going into battle.

Downfall

Beginning in 1350, Thai armies started a series of attacks on the Khmers that would last for 80 years. During this time, expensive building projects were costing the Khmers a lot of money, and this meant they had less money for wars. There were also leadership struggles within the royal family, and this meant that the rulers had to put energy into keeping themselves in power rather than fighting the enemies of the empire. In 1431 the Thais captured Angkor and looted Angkor Wat. The beautiful city was abandoned, and the Khmer empire collapsed.
It survived as a small kingdom until 1863, when the French took control of Cambodia.

War Elephants

The Khmers were fierce warriors, and they trained elephants to help them defeat their enemies. War elephants might have their tusks fitted with spikes or blades. They also wore armour, probably made of chain mail (steel rings linked together), leather, quilted fabric, or bamboo. In addition to the driver, war elephants could carry two or three warriors armed with bows, darts, or fiery missiles. Clanging bells and gongs were used to terrify their enemies as the Khmers attacked. Using these methods, the Khmers were able to control Southeast Asia from the 9th century until the mid-14th century.

45

India

Hinduism

Hinduism and Buddhism both arose in ancient India, and have millions of followers today. Hinduism is one of the oldest religions in the world – its origins go back over 4,000 years. Hindus believe all living things have souls and are on a journey towards God. This means being born again and again in different forms. In each lifetime

Hindus believe in many gods. On the left is the river goddess Ganga; on the right is Indra, the god of war and thunder.

we have to deal with the results of our actions in earlier lives. This is like cleaning a house after thoughtlessly making a mess. Life by life, the past can be cleaned up.

Hindus believe that there are many gods, just as there are many different creatures. Over all, there are three Hindu gods: Brahma, the creator; Vishnu, the protector of the world; and Shiva, the destroyer. Everything that exists goes through these three stages.

The most sacred books of Hinduism are the Vedas, hymns on which the religion is based, and the Upanishads.

Buddhism

Buddhism arose from the teaching of one extraordinary man, Siddhartha, who lived from about 560 to 480 BC. He taught not about a god, but about the human journey. He also taught that we live again and again, and have the chance in each life to sort out mistakes we made in past lives.

Above all, Siddhartha taught that we should be kind and good to others. He also pointed out that in life everything changes all the time. According to Buddhist beliefs, you should not get too worked up about happiness or sadness, or about anything, but instead focus simply on becoming wise.

The Buddhist teachings spread throughout India, and from there to Tibet, China, Japan, and Southeast Asia. However, by the 13th century AD Buddhism had almost died out completely in India.

Islam

Islam was founded in Arabia in the 7th century AD by the prophet Muhammad, and spread rapidly. Soon Muslim raiders reached India in search of wealth. But Islam had little impact there until around the year 1000. From 1001 to 1026 a Turkish Muslim warrior king, Mahmud, repeatedly invaded northern India, destroying Hindu temples and stripping them of their treasures. Using this wealth Mahmud made the Afghan city of Ghazni into a great Islamic centre.

Many more Muslim attackers came from Afghanistan and Central Asia in the next centuries. They were mostly Turkish peoples, and devastated many

A statue of Siddhartha Gautama, the Buddha, or 'Enlightened One'.

Hindu temples and sacred places, and sometimes attacked Buddhists too. Muslims were far better organized as soldiers than Hindus, and by 1200 the whole of northern India had fallen to Islam, after a series of campaigns by another Muslim ruler, Muhammad of Ghur. However, further south in India, out of reach of Muslim armies, Hindu kingdoms survived. In 1336 some of these were brought together in a great Hindu empire, called Vijayanagar, which was to dominate southern India for another two centuries.

In the north, the most important Muslim state was the Sultanate of Delhi. Over the next century its power increased and by 1300 it was at a peak of prosperity and power. Its influence reached far beyond its borders, and it was strong enough to repel attacks from invading Mongols in the early 14th century. It was eventually overthrown in 1526 by another wave of Muslim invaders from Afghanistan, the Moguls.

Mathematics

Without the brilliance of Indian mathematicians, modern mathematics as we know it could not exist. Indians introduced nought, or zero, as a 'number'. They also developed the idea of using the position of a digit in a number to show its value. The difference between 10 and 1,000, or 23 and 230, is only obvious because of the Indian system.

Tantrism

Tantrism, or Tantra, arose within both Buddhism and Hinduism. In tantrism the union of opposites, such as male and female, is important. Tantric rituals involve yoga, with the use of special postures, breathing exercises, and meditation.

Islands of the Pacific

Hundreds of years before the invention of the compass, the people of the Pacific Ocean islands of Polynesia sailed vast distances to settle in the remote islands of the Pacific. Their expert knowledge of the stars and ocean currents helped them navigate. They also used fluorescent algae and the patterns of migrating birds to guide them on the highways of the sea. These skilled sailors travelled in canoes made of hollowed tree trunks, some up to 100 metres (330 feet) long.

Hawaii

The Polynesians reached the islands of Hawaii in about AD 400. In this tropical paradise, the

A Maori mask carved from wood. The person represented by the mask can be identified by the unique pattern of the tattoos shown on it.

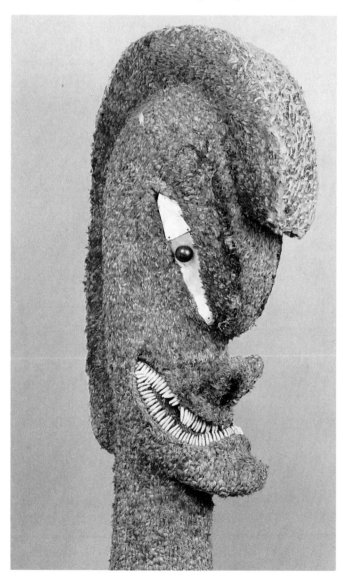

The Hawaiian war god Kakailimokum. This has been made using a variety of materials, including wickerwork and feathers.

Tattoos

Both men and women are tattooed in the Maori culture. The tattoos show a person's rank as well as his or her ancestry, skills, and achievements. Tattooing is done by using an albatross bone to chisel lines and curves into the skin. A dye made of soot and dog fat is rubbed into the skin to add colour. Maori women who hold sacred knowledge or are very high in rank received a tattoo that makes it clear they will marry only men with high rankings.

Moa is the Maori word for the giant flightless birds that were once common in New Zealand. The largest species grew up to 2.5 metres (8 feet) tall and may have weighed over 250 kilograms (550 pounds) – quite a feast for the Maoris. They were hunted for food, and their bones and eggshells were used as tools and ornaments. By the 18th century the moas had become extinct, probably because they were so heavily hunted and because the grasses, leaves, berries, and seeds they fed on were increasingly cleared away.

The skull of a moa. There were 13 different species of moa in New Zealand, ranging in size from around 1 to 3 metres, before people arrived there. All are now extinct.

settlers became accomplished fishers and farmers. The islands were each ruled by their own king and quarrels among them were not unusual, but the small numbers of fighting men on any island made long-term wars impossible. In the 11th century an army of Tahitians took over the Hawaiian islands and introduced a complex system of rules and regulations called *kapu*. This made it possible for the Tahitians to dominate Hawaii for 100 years, after which they suddenly abandoned the islands, never to return.

Maoris Arrive in New Zealand

It is unclear when Polynesian settlers first came to New Zealand. There is evidence that visits were made over 1,000 years ago, but the main immigrations were between about AD 960 and 1400. The settlers, called Maoris, named the land Aotearoa, the land of the long white cloud.

Toi-Te-Huatahi, from Tahiti, was one of the earliest recorded visitors to New Zealand. He went there in the 11th century to search for his grandson Whatonga. Whatonga had been lost at sea during an inter-island canoe race, but he somehow managed to stay alive and make it

Aborigines of Australia

The native inhabitants of Australia, the Aborigines, are thought to have travelled there from Indonesia over 50,000 years ago, but Europeans did not visit the continent until the 17th century. The Aborigines had no formal government. Instead, their society was organized into family units with strict laws and well-defined responsibilities. The Dreamtime, which was the Aboriginal story of creation, was told through stories, art, songs, and dances. Individuals were taught to value and respect others, as they were only one part of a long pattern of life and relationships. The knowledge of Dreamtime, which binds individuals together before birth, during life, and after death, was passed from generation to generation.

back to Tahiti. There he heard of his grandfather's expedition, and he returned to Aotearoa to find him. After a long and difficult search, the two were finally reunited.

The climate in Aotearoa was cooler and wetter than the Polynesians were used to. Of the crops they brought with them only the taro, yam and sweet potato would grow, but they soon discovered other types of food including small reptiles, edible ferns, shellfish, and the moa, a giant flightless bird.

Civilization in the Americas

Many civilizations existed in North and South America long before European explorers travelled there. Early Americans farmed the land and built towns, palaces, and temples. Many of these peoples specialized in crafts, particularly pottery and carving.

An Anasazi pitcher dating from around the beginning of the 12th-century. It is about 20 centimetres in height.

The Mississippi Mound-builders

The Mississippian culture developed around the Mississippi River. It was at its most advanced around 1000 and spread across what is now the middle and southeast of the USA. The Mississippi people were farmers, who mostly grew maize, beans, and squashes. They lived in towns and villages ruled by priests. Each town had separate family houses, a central plaza (open area) used for ceremonies, and a temple on top of an enormous mound made of earth in the shape of a pyramid or oval. In their main city of

Cahokia, in what is now the state of Illinois, the mound was 300 metres (1,000 feet) long, 200 metres (700 feet) wide, and 30 metres (100 feet) high.

One of the features of the Mississippi culture was its art. Craftsmen carved elaborate designs, including serpents, spiders, and human faces, into copper, stone, wood, and clay, and made fancy headdresses and masks. The Mississippi culture lasted until European explorers reached the area at the end of the 17th century.

The Anasazi Cliff Dwellers

The Anasazi (which means 'ancient ones' in the Navajo language) lived in the southwest of what is now the USA from around AD 100. They built huge mud-brick homes with interconnecting rooms. These were like early blocks of flats, and as more of them were built they grew into small communities called pueblos. These communities were on the valley floor. In around 1050 the Anasazi moved into the hills and began to build stone pueblos

These carved columns were originally used to support a 12th-century Toltec temple. They may have represented great warriors or leaders.

50

Mesa Verde

The Anasazi built a pueblo in southwestern Colorado that still exists today. It is now called Mesa Verde (Spanish for 'green table') after the thick forests that cover its flat top. Among its impressive cliff dwellings is the Cliff Palace in Cliff Canyon, which contains hundreds of rooms and kivas. Anasazi people lived at Mesa Verde until the end of the 13th century, when something – perhaps a drought – caused them to move.

into the sides of cliffs. These were better, as they offered protection from enemies and harsh weather conditions. The Pueblo Native Americans who live in the same area today are descendants of the Anasazi.

At the base of their cliff dwellings, the Anasazi built underground ceremonial rooms called kivas. These were round, with a bench around the inside wall and a ladder to get in and out. Only men were allowed inside.

The Toltecs

The Toltecs established an empire in what is now Mexico during the 10th century. They built their capital at Tula. They had a strong army and were successful in war, enlarging their empire by defeating neighbouring peoples. Their religion was based on the worship of gods that were represented by animals. Their main god was Quetzalcoatl, the feathered serpent, which they worshipped as the god of the planet Venus. Ruins at Tula, which was about 80 kilometres (50 miles) north of Mexico City, include three pyramid temples, one of which is thought to be dedicated to Quetzalcoatl. The Toltec were also talented

craftspeople, particularly noted for their fine metalwork and enormous statues of humans and animals. Their culture lasted until around the mid-12th century, when invaders, including the Aztec people, destroyed their capital.

The Chimu Kingdom

The Chimu people lived in South America from about the 12th century and created a powerful kingdom in the first half of the 14th century. Their capital was at Chan Chan, in Peru, and they lived along the northern Pacific coast. Chan Chan contained large rectangular compounds where the important lords lived with their families and servants. The city was surrounded by a 9-metre (30-feet) wall. People in Chan Chan had plenty to eat because the Chimu had an excellent system of irrigation to water their crops. Chimu craftspeople specialized in pottery and weaving. They thrived until the 15th century, when they were conquered by the Incas

The Start of the Crusades

Retaking the Holy Land

Of all the cities on earth mentioned in the Bible, Jerusalem is the most famous and important. It is a very holy place for Jews and Christians. From 638, however, Arab Muslims had been in control of the city, and had built some of their own holy mosques there. They still let people of other religions come and worship, though.

In 1071 a people from Turkey called the Seljuks invaded the Holy Land. They were also Muslims, but rough and warlike, and attacked Christians who came on pilgrimage. To make things worse, they took over the Church of the Holy Sepulchre, which is built on the spot where Jesus is thought to have been crucified. Christians were upset about this and also worried that the Turks would soon come and conquer Constantinople (now called Istanbul, in modern Turkey), the centre of Eastern Christianity and of the Greek Byzantine Empire.

In November 1095 Pope Urban II spoke to a meeting of church leaders near Clermont in France. He called on Frenchmen to go and save the Greek Christians who had been invaded by the Turks. He also told them to free Jerusalem,

Pope Urban II speaks to a meeting of church leaders in 1095. He called for a crusade to free Jerusalem from the Muslims.

especially the Church of the Holy Sepulchre. To his surprise, people began to cry out, 'God wills it! God wills it!' They knelt down at his feet to show that they were ready to go right away.

The Pope and other leaders went on preaching this message through France and Germany. Many more people, from poor and uneducated villagers to rich nobles, from simple pilgrims to bishops and priests, also agreed to go on this great journey to free Jerusalem. This was the start of the crusades.

Forgiven Sins

Pilgrimages to the Holy Land were already very popular. People could see and touch the places where holy things had happened, and were promised that some of their sins would be forgiven if they went. Now, the Pope announced that all the sins of the crusaders would be wiped out! This made crusading even more popular.

A Dangerous Journey

None of the people who volunteered to go on this long trek had much of an idea of what was before them. It would mean 3,200 kilometres (2,000 miles) of travelling, for some on horseback, for others on foot. It would take years, and might cost them everything they owned. There would be no way to contact those they left at home, and no way of knowing whether or not they would make it back alive.

Godfrey of Bouillon leads the capture of Jerusalem in 1099 at the end of the First Crusade.

Cross Wearers

The people who decided to go and fight the Muslims tore pieces of red cloth into crosses and sewed them onto their clothes. This gives us the word crusaders, which comes from the Latin word for cross.

and attacking Jews. Most of them died before they even got to Constantinople, but the rest were killed by the Turks just beyond Constantinople, near Nicaea (modern Iznik in Turkey), leaving behind a huge mountain of bones.

The First Crusade

Meanwhile, a large army was preparing to set out for the Holy Land. These soldiers arrived in Jerusalem in 1099 after more than two years of travelling. They conquered Antioch, an important trading town, along the way. They built siege machines out of wood to break down the strong walls of Jerusalem. Finally they broke through, slaughtering the Muslims with their swords and burning a synagogue full of Jews. They rejoiced that they had recaptured the city, and chose one of their leaders, Godfrey of Bouillon, Duke of Lorraine, as king of Jerusalem – but there were more battles to come.

The Peasants' Crusade

The first person to lead a crusade was a man called Peter the Hermit. With a dirty woollen hood surrounding his long face, he was said to look like the donkey he rode on! In 1096 more than 300,000 people, mainly peasants, were persuaded by his preaching to march to Jerusalem. But Peter was not a strong leader and the crusaders got out of control, burning palaces

Peter the Hermit addresses a few of those who followed him in the ill-fated Peasants' Crusade.

The End of the Crusades

The Second Crusade

Between the 11th and 14th centuries there were many crusades, some more famous than others. The First Crusaders had trouble keeping control of Jerusalem once it had been captured. In 1144 the crusader city of Edessa (modern Urfa in Turkey) was captured by Muslims, which put Jerusalem in danger again. A Second

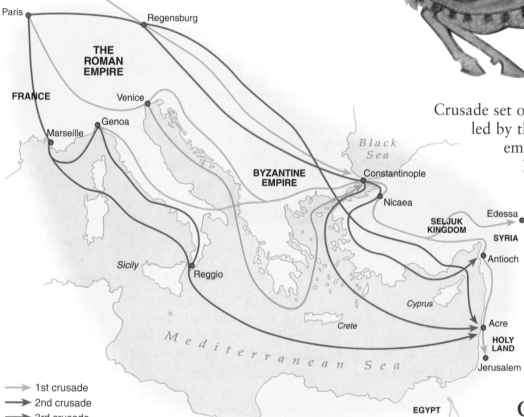

Crusade set out three years later, led by the Holy Roman emperor and the king of France. Like many other crusaders, they had terrible troubles on the journey, lost the battles with the Muslims (or Saracens, as they were often called), and had to retreat.

The Third Crusade

After this disaster, there wasn't another crusade for 40 years. But in 1187 Saladin, the sultan of Egypt and Syria, recaptured Jerusalem for the Muslims. It was said that Pope Urban III died of shock when he heard about it. A Third Crusade set off

Why Crusade?

One reason why crusades became popular is that some people were looking for fame, riches, and adventure. If they won a great battle, they would be called heroes. Others decided to go as an act of faith in God.

Once someone made a vow to take the cross (promise to go on the crusade), they might not be allowed to change their mind. Even if they died, one of their children might have to go in their place. At first women were not allowed, except washerwomen, but later, nuns, wives, and other women went on crusades.

Bernard of Clairvaux (1090-1153)

Bernard was the abbot (leader) of a monastery in Clairvaux, France. In 1147 he urged Christians to go on the Second Crusade, saying: 'Why are you delaying, servants of the cross, you who have great physical strength and many wordly goods? I advise you not to put your own business before the business of Christ'.

King Richard the Lionheart of England (on the right) battles with Saladin, a great Muslim warrior who recaptured Jerusalem from the Crusaders.

for the Holy Land, this time headed by King Philip II of France, the German emperor Frederick Barbarossa, and Richard the Lionheart of England. This crusade also went badly, with arguments between the leaders. Barbarossa was drowned before he even got to the Holy Land, and some of his soldiers went home. In 1191, however, by using a giant catapult, they managed to capture the city of Acre (now in northern Israel), although they were not able to recapture Jerusalem.

The Fourth Crusade

Eight years later Pope Innocent III called for another crusade. The Fourth Crusade set off in 1202, but most of the soldiers never even got to the Holy Land. Instead, they ended up attacking Constantinople (modern Istanbul in Turkey), the centre of Eastern Christianity and capital of the Byzantine Empire. The crusaders got rich from all the treasure when they looted the city, but many people were disgusted by their greed.

The armies of the Fourth Crusade never reached the Holy Land. Instead they attacked and looted the Christian city of Constantinople.

The End of the Crusades

Life for crusaders was very hard. There were no maps to guide them and not enough food. Many people died of starvation, thirst, and disease, as well as from war, and their families were left alone. People started to protest at the violence and waste of lives, and to say the crusades were a bad thing. By 1300 the main crusades came to an end. More crusaders went out, but they never regained Jerusalem.

Discoveries and Inventions

During the Middle Ages many people could not read or write, and had to work so hard to survive that they didn't have much of a chance to think about science or invent clever things. In some monasteries, however, it was a different story. These monasteries had great libraries, where some of the monks studied ancient manuscripts (hand-written books) and learned about the past. Monks also did experiments with growing plants and made discoveries about medicine.

Meanwhile, as lots of people travelled on pilgrimages and crusades, they discovered things that were already known about in other parts of the world. If they were not killed or taken prisoner and managed to make it back to Europe, they brought with them some of the ideas and customs of the Arab countries, where society was more advanced in many ways. For

Clocks

Although the Chinese invented a mechanical clock before 1100, they did not develop it further, and based later clocks on the ones invented in Europe. By 1300 different European inventors had made mechanical clocks driven by weights. They had no hands, but a chiming bell told the hour. By around 1350 clocks had a dial and an hour hand.

example, the Arabs had a better way of writing numbers – and this is the way we write them today. But many of the technological marvels of the Arab world – such as paper – had been invented in China centuries before. Unfortunately, because of lack of communication, it was a long time before the common people of Europe got the benefit of some of these great ideas.

Important Inventions

Approximate Date	Discovery or Invention	Where
11th century	chimney	Central Europe
11th century	mills using tidal power	France
11th century	spiral staircase	Europe
1080	movable windmill, (able to turn in the wind)	Europe
1040–50	movable type (for printing)	China
1088	magnetic needle compass	China
1150	longbow	Wales
1200	spinning wheel	India
1266	magnifying glass	England
1310	mechanical clocks	Europe
1320	cannon	Europe

The cannon was the first firearm to be invented in Europe. It is not known where or when the first one was built.

Roger Bacon (about 1214–about 1294)

Roger Bacon was born in Somerset, England, around 1214 and studied at the universities of Oxford and Paris. He became a Franciscan friar, but because he taught that people should experiment and think things out for themselves, the church ordered him to stop teaching, and even locked him up in a convent in Paris. The church thought such views could be dangerous, as people might question all the things the church taught. However, Pope Clement IV was a friend of Bacon's, and encouraged him to write down what he knew.

Bacon had many original ideas about science, philosophy, and technology. He believed that mathematics is the key to many discoveries. He also thought studying languages and the scientific knowledge of other cultures was important. Some of his greatest discoveries were in optics, the study of light. He studied rainbows, invented lenses for magnifying glasses, and described how to build a telescope.

Bacon also had ideas about a flying machine called an ornithopter, hot-air balloons, and gunpowder. He guessed that in the future people would travel quickly in carriages without horses, and in ships without rowers. That seemed impossible at the time. Only in the 20th century have people realized how great Bacon was.

A 14th-century illustration showing a spinning wheel. The spinning wheel was invented in India and first appeared in Europe in the 14th century.

The invention of the longbow was a revolution in warfare. Its arrows could penetrate plate armour at close range.

Alchemy

Alchemy was a craft that involved magical powers. It had been practised from ancient times. The alchemists aimed to turn 'base' metals such as iron or lead into gold, and also tried to discover the 'elixir of life', a substance that would keep people young forever. Although none of them succeeded, alchemists in the Middle Ages did develop a lot of equipment that is still used by chemists today, and they also discovered pure alcohol and several kinds of acid.

Everyday Life in Towns

Offa, an 8th-century king of England, directs the building of a monastery in honour of St Alban.

New Towns

In the Middle Ages many new towns were built. Towns grew up alongside rivers or at crossroads, where travellers would pass. They were often built near a castle or monastery, because it was safer from attack and lots of people could get jobs there. Quite often, the ground was wet and boggy and would have to be drained before the gravel or cobblestone streets could be laid. The people who bought plots of land to build on would have to dig their own wells, latrines (outside toilets), and rubbish pits, and as time went on the ground and water usually got smelly and polluted.

Most medieval towns were very small, more like the size of modern villages. In Britain, London was by far the biggest town. Most people were still living and working in the countryside, and even townspeople might keep animals and farm land outside the town walls.

If the king gave a town a royal charter, the townspeople had special permission to make their own rules and hold markets. In those

Clothes

In the Middle Ages it was easy to tell rich from poor people. The clothes of the rich were ankle-length, grandly decorated, and made from expensive materials. Fur, from the skins of different animals, including cats, and shoes with long, pointed toes were considered very fashionable.

Peasants wore shorter clothes made from coarse woollen or linen cloth, and sometimes sheepskin or leather. They dressed in dull colours. Some were so poor that they went barefoot, but others wore leather boots or clogs (wooden shoes).

Craftspeople were somewhere in the middle. Women always wore their skirts long and covered their heads. They would strap pattens (overshoes with wooden soles) to their shoes to keep them clean when walking on the muddy streets.

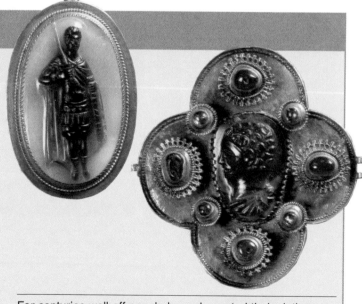

For centuries well-off people have decorated their clothes with expensive jewellery.

times, each town was completely separate from other towns, and people were more loyal to their town than to their country. Strong stone walls or wooden stockades were built to keep out any outsiders. At night, the gate was closed and people would only be let in if the keeper decided that they were friends, not enemies.

Town Houses

There wasn't very much room inside town walls for building new houses. Each plot of land had a narrow end facing out onto the street. Usually the ground floor was a shop, and the owners lived upstairs with their servants sleeping higher up in the attics. As time went on, people might build extra rooms or storeys. Because there wasn't much room at the back or sides, town houses often had rooms that jutted out from the upper storeys over the streets. This made the streets below even more dark and narrow.

Queen Isabella arrives in Paris. She would live in much greater comfort than most people in 14th-century Europe.

Fire!

Fire was a terrible risk in towns, because so many wooden houses were built so close together. At nightfall, the curfew bell was rung, warning people to go inside and cover up their fires so that they would not set the chimneys alight. A night watchman would prowl around the streets looking for signs of sparks. If a house was on fire, the only cure was to pull it down, so that the whole town would not catch fire.

Marriage

Girls could get married as young as 12 years old, but boys from craftsmen's families had to wait until they had finished being an apprentice. Usually a girl's father would choose her husband for her, and would try to make a good business deal for himself at the same time. He would have to pay a dowry – a gift of money, furniture, or other things – to the husband. A rich family could afford a big dowry. If a woman's husband died, she might be able to take over her husband's business, but otherwise things could be very hard for a poor widow.

59

Markets and Fairs

Guilds

In the 11th and 12th centuries the people who worked in towns were mainly traders, craftsmen, and their helpers. They joined together in unions called guilds, which made rules about how good their products had to be, trained apprentices, gave out sick pay and pensions, and kept outsiders from trying to take their business.

People could only join a guild if they paid a fee each year, and if their work was good enough. Even though women did many jobs such as brewing ale, keeping shops, baking, spinning, or weaving silk, they were hardly ever allowed to join the guilds. Each town had its own guilds, and usually there would be separate guilds for different trades. They often clustered together in one street. Tailors, for example, might be on Threadneedle Street, and candlemakers on Chandler Street. Officials called wardens checked up on the guild members and made them pay a fine if they made bad goods.

Guilds were an important part of town life. Some were mainly religious and did charity work. They also paid priests to say prayers for the members. Grand 'guildhalls' were built for

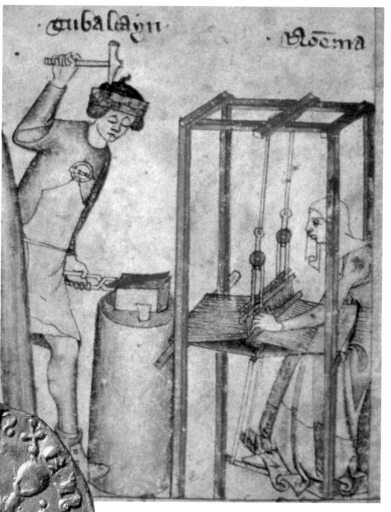

Metalworking and weaving were two of the crafts skills that were in demand in medieval times.

A 13th-century gold penny. Many people exchanged goods and services rather than paying for them.

their meetings, and guilds held parades where they would wear special guild livery (costumes).

Craftspeople

In medieval times common tradespeople included hosiers (stockingmakers), glove and shoemakers, bakers and piemakers (most

---

Apprentices

Young boys started out their working lives as apprentices, when their fathers paid for them to live with a master craftsman in his shop and learn all the tricks of his trade. The apprentice had to do any job the master gave him without pay. After about seven years he could become a journeyman (a qualified craftsman), and perhaps one day a master. First, though, he would have to make a fine example of his work, called a masterpiece, so that the guild could judge whether he was good enough to become a master.

Market Day

The high points of town life were the markets and fairs. Markets usually happened once a week, so that people could get together to sell or trade their goods. Sometimes separate markets were held for different types of produce, for example just to sell meat or butter. Village people would walk into the towns to sell their spare eggs, chickens, cheese, wool, or grain at little stalls. While they were at the fair they might be able to trade these goods for things like shoes, cloth, and cooking pans that they couldn't make themselves. Merchants might come from further away with more exotic goods, travelling by water or using packhorses and carts.

An illustration of a fair in medieval France. A fair could last for several weeks.

townspeople didn't have their own ovens), grocers, metal workers and armourmakers, and leather tanners. There were also many people who worked with cloth: fullers (who pounded and washed cloth to make it stronger), dyers, spinners, weavers, mercers (people dealing in fabrics), tailors, and embroiderers. All these people might show their goods at the markets and fairs.

Fun of the Fair

A fair was like a market, but it was much bigger and usually happened only once a year. Luxuries such as furs, silks, wine, and spices might be sold. Although, like the market, the main purpose of the fair was for buying and selling goods or hiring workers, it was also a great time for having fun. Exciting entertainers such as acrobats, jesters telling rude jokes, musicians, and dancing bears might all be seen in the crowded, noisy streets. Lots of eating (foods like meat pies and toffee apples) and drinking went on as people played dice games or bet on wrestling matches and cock fights. Some fairs went on for a long time – weeks, or even months!

Some of the biggest fairs have lasted to this day, such as the St Bartholomew Fair in London and the St Giles Fair in Oxford, but now they are just for fun and entertainment.

Trade Routes

Merchants

In the early Middle Ages travelling salespeople or peddlers wandered from town to town, buying and selling things. Gradually, people in Europe became richer and had more things to trade for other things they wanted. Merchants were able to earn their living by going to parts of the world that most people never saw, and bringing back goods that could not be found in their home country. Sometimes a merchant would pay other people to do the travelling. Traders carried bills of exchange – like traveller's cheques – instead of large sums of money, so they would not be robbed.

Merchants were able to make a profit at fairs and markets by selling valuable things that people were not able to make in their own towns and villages. Some of the most famous of these fairs were held in Champagne, France, and Stourbridge, England. Rich people and monasteries would send their servants to buy goods at the fairs, where they would stock up on a year's supply of salt, spices, wine, and other foods, and sometimes luxuries such as silk fabrics.

The crusades had made trading with the East easier, and increased peoples' appetites for foreign foods – crusaders had brought back not only exotic spices, but recipes too! Some merchants got very rich through trading, and so did the money lenders who did the job of banks. This angered some people, who thought that only noble landowners should be wealthy.

This 15th-century illustration shows traders bringing goods to the Gulf of Cambay in India.

Trading Cities

Italy was the greatest trading centre in Europe at this time, with huge fleets of merchant ships. Some of the Italian cities became so big and important that they were called city-states, because they were as powerful as states by themselves. Venice, Pisa, and Genoa were three of the greatest and, like countries, they sometimes went to war with each other.

In Germany trading towns got together and formed a union called the Hanseatic League. Their aim was to help each other fight pirates and bandits, and to gain control of all the foreign trade. The League became very powerful and traded as far away as Russia and Iceland.

Jewish Traders

As moneylenders, the Jews were very important to trade and the economy. Their moneylending activities made them very unpopular. Some people were suspicious of them, and jealous that they made so much money. In many parts of Europe, Jewish communities were attacked from time to time, and many Jewish people were killed. In 1290 King Edward I found out that he could borrow money from the Italian banks instead of from the Jews. He made all the Jews leave Britain, and they weren't allowed to live there again for hundreds of years.

Trade Routes

Cargo ships were used to carry heavy loads across long distances. Even though sea travel was slow, it was usually safer and easier than going by land. Italian cargo ships would buy luxuries such as gold, silks, and spices from the East, and trade them for valuable goods from England and Flanders (modern Belgium), such as wool and coal.

What Everyone Wanted

Everyone was eager to have goods that were difficult to find in their own country.

Goods	Came From
silk, spices	Far East
oranges, lemons	Mediterranean
leather	Spain
almonds	Greece
fine clothes, jewellery	Italy
linen, metal armour	Germany
wine, honey, beeswax	France
cloth	Flanders (modern Belgium)
furs, timber, fish	Scandinavia
wool	England
cheese	Netherlands
furs	Russia
slaves	Eastern Europe

Constantinople

Antioch

Caspian Sea

Samarkand

Kashgar

CHINA

Canton

INDIA

The Silk Road, linking the Pacific and the Mediterranean.

German and Dutch ships carried timber, iron, copper, and lead south to the Mediterranean, and brought back wine, oil, and salt.

Goods from Asia could be transported over deserts along the ancient Silk Road by camel caravans, or by water from India to the Red Sea and then overland to the Mediterranean. Silk was traded for European goods such as cloth, furs, hides, iron, linen, timber, and even slaves.

Great camel trains carried goods and traders across the vast distances of central Asia.

Travellers and Explorers

Travel was difficult in the Middle Ages, but there were many great travellers. Some were merchants, who travelled as far as India and China for valuables such as silk and spices. Some were pilgrims: Christians travelling to Jerusalem, or Muslims going to Mecca. A few travelled simply because they loved it. Travellers' accounts of their journeys captured the imaginations of later explorers such as Christopher Columbus.

A scene showing the departure of Marco Polo from Venice at the beginning of his epic travels. It was painted some years after Marco's death.

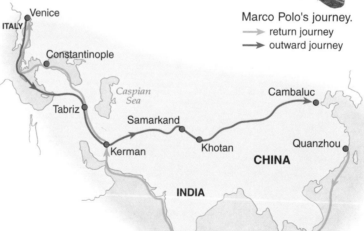

Marco Polo's journey.
→ return journey
→ outward journey

Venice
ITALY
Constantinople
Caspian Sea
Tabriz
Kerman
Samarkand
Khotan
Cambaluc
Quanzhou
CHINA
INDIA

Marco Polo

Marco Polo was born in Venice in about 1254. His father and uncle were both well-travelled merchants. In 1271 they set out on a trip to the court of Kublai Khan, the Mongol emperor of China, and 17-year-old Marco went with them. From Hormuz in Persia they intended to travel by ship, but they found no ships fit for a long sea voyage. Instead they travelled overland, through the desert regions of Persia (modern Iran) and the valleys of northern Afghanistan, across the Pamir Mountains, then east to Kublai Khan's summer palace at Shang-tu.

Travelling Troubles

Travelling in the Middle Ages was slow and difficult. On land, the most comfortable way to travel was in a litter (a vehicle containing a couch) carried by servants, but this was only for the very rich. Most people walked or rode horses or camels. For long journeys travel by sea was most comfortable, but there were still hazards. Boats were at the mercy of the wind, and there were no charts for navigating in unknown waters.

Kublai Khan was impressed by Marco and gave him a job in government. He sent the young man on many journeys to report on distant parts of his vast empire. Eventually, in 1292, the Polos set off home, travelling by ship, then by land. They arrived back in Venice in 1295, after 24 years away. Marco Polo later wrote a book about his adventures. Most people didn't believe his amazing tales.

Ibn Battuta

Probably the greatest traveller of the period was Ibn Battuta, a Muslim from Tangier in North Africa. At 21 he made a pilgrimage to Mecca, and discovered he loved to travel. He travelled for several years around Iran, Iraq, and Arabia, then in 1332 he decided to visit India. His route took him through Egypt and Syria, Turkey, southern Russia, and Afghanistan. He eventually reached Delhi, where the sultan made him an important official. However, he was always in fear of losing favour and being put to death, so in 1342 he left on a trip to China. He was shipwrecked on the way and travelled for several years before eventually reaching China from Sumatra in a new ship. After nearly 30 years of travelling, Battuta at last decided to go home. He arrived in 1349, and made only one further trip in his life, across the Sahara Desert to Timbuktu in West Africa. He dictated the story of his travels, which in 30 years had taken him over 120,000 kilometres (72,000 miles) – more than four times further than Marco Polo.

The Wonders of Cathay

In his account of his travels in Cathay (China), Marco Polo describes how in many ways Chinese civilization was more advanced than that of Europe at that time. He travelled on great Chinese sea-going junks (flat-bottomed sailing boats), which were far superior to European ships of the period. He also described how the Chinese used coal for heating (coal was not used in Europe for another 400 years). But, astonishingly, he did not mention China's most obvious landmark – the Great Wall.

Travelling was slow in medieval times. There were few good roads and people went on foot or, if they were wealthy enough, on horseback or by boat.

The Stories of John Mandeville

Sir John Mandeville was an English knight who in the 1350s published a book, *The Travels of Sir John Mandeville.* It is not clear whether Mandeville himself travelled at all, despite the book's title; most of his stories were taken from other books of the time. Many of the places he wrote about, such as the land of Prester John, did not exist. Later explorers found that most of Mandeville's tales were untrue, but his entertaining book remained popular.

Empires of West Africa

During the Middle Ages, West Africa was dominated in turn by three great empires. They were very, very wealthy, because they had so much gold. They were also well organized and relatively peaceful.

The Ghana Empire

The first of these empires was Ghana. (The modern country of Ghana has taken its name from it.) Its origins are unclear but most people were Mande. The empire flourished, between the 8th and 11th centuries, trading gold and ivory with Arabs and Berbers to the north, and salt with the peoples to the south. In 1067 a visiting Arab writer recorded that the Ghanaian army numbered 200,000 men, 40,000 of them archers.

The Berbers were a groups of people who lived in the western Sahara. They founded the city of Marrakech, which became one of the greatest cities of North Africa. A powerful group of Muslim Berbers called the Almoravids, and led by AbuBakr, moved south to invade the Ghana empire and convert its people to Islam. Kumbi, the capital of the Ghana empire, was captured in 1076 and, with the dominance of the Almoravids, the Ghana empire fell into decline.

The Mali Empire

As the Ghana empire became weaker and started to break up, it was ruled by the both Keita people and the Susa people. In 1230 Sun Diata, the Keita leader won a great victory over the Susa and founded the Mali empire, which became even larger and more powerful than the Ghana empire had been. The increase in sea exploration and trading voyages from Europe, the Middle East, and China spread the fame of the empire of Mali. Many traders and travellers told of its wealth and splendour. Mali gained its wealth because it had control of the trade routes across the Sahara desert. It took taxes from merchants carrying gold, silver, and ivory through to the North African coast, en route to Europe.

Gold has always been highly prized, and the people of Mali had more than most.

The Mande eventually opened up trading routes in many directions. To the east, they extended as far as the Hausa states near the River Niger and Lake Chad. To the south they reached the coast (in modern Ghana), where more gold was being mined. The wealth of the Mande increased as they obtained gold and other precious materials for themselves. There were many prosperous cities in the region, the best known being Timbuktu. The most famous ruler of Mali was Mansa Musa.

Mediterranean Sea

Fez

Tripoli

S A H A R A

Timbuktu

Niger

Gulf of Guinea

—— trade route
⬭ Ghana empire
⬭ Mali empire
⬭ Songhai empire

The Songhai Empire

The third empire to gain power in the region started in the 15th century. Its rulers, the Songhai, were already a strong and independent people under the Mande. They controlled fishing and water transport on much of the River Niger, and it was never easy for the Mande to control them. The Songhai reached the peak of their power in the 15th and 16th centuries, when they formed a largely Muslim empire. They controlled most of the trade across the Sahara, and become very wealthy, surviving until 1590 when the empire fell to Moroccan invaders.

These Tuaregs from Algeria belong to the Berber people, the original peoples of North Africa. The Almoravids were also Berbers.

Mansa Musa's Trip to Mecca

Mansa Musa, the king of Mali between 1312 and 1337, was known for his great wealth and the splendour of his court. He was a Muslim, and in 1324 he made a pilgrimage to Mecca, the holiest city for Muslims. With him he took 60,000 people and 150 kilograms (330 pounds) of gold. Every Friday (the Muslim holy day) he stopped to pray. He had a mosque built in every place he stopped.

On the way, Mansa Musa spent some time in Cairo, the capital of Egypt. While he was there he presented gifts of gold to almost everybody in the city. The Egyptians obtained more gold from him in trading exchanges. As a result, a huge amount of gold circulated throughout Egypt. The value of the Egyptian currency dropped sharply with so much gold about. It remained weak for over 12 years after Mansa Musa's visit.

Kingdoms and Religions of Africa

Travellers' Tales

Many Arab travellers wrote about the African kingdoms they visited. One of these travellers was Ibn Battuta. Around 1350, he told of the splendour of the Malian king, who held court dressed in red velvet and gold, on a silk carpet, with a silk canopy over him. Musicians with gold and silver instruments played for him and he was waited on by over 300 slaves.

Battuta was shocked at the fact that the African women went around completely naked. He also said that, above all peoples, the black Africans hated injustice. It was always punished. Because of this, travellers were completely safe there. Even if a traveller died in the kingdom, his goods were kept safely by the people until a friend or relative came to claim them.

Great Zimbabwe

The interior of Africa was rich in metals of all sorts. In addition to gold, copper and iron were of huge importance in the development of stable societies throughout the continent.

Across southern Africa are the ruins of many impressive settlements which were built and grew strong in the period known as the Late Iron Age in that area (beginning about AD1). The best known of these is Great Zimbabwe. The modern country of Zimbabwe is named after it. The name 'Zimbabwe' means 'stone building'. The buildings of Great Zimbabwe date from the 8th to the 17th centuries

Great Zimbabwe was the capital of the Shona people, who became rich from trading gold. The city was made up of massive stone buildings, some of them royal burial places. The stones used to construct the buildings were shaped to fit together perfectly. The people who did this must have been extremely skilled craftsmen, with advanced mathematical and engineering abilities. An oval building in the centre was the main living area. There were also pillars made of soapstone, carved with birds which probably had a religious meaning. The ruins of Great Zimbabwe are preserved today as a World Heritage Site.

The site of Great Zimbabwe was first occupied around AD400. The ruins there now date from the 14th century, when it was rebuilt following a fire.

Religion in Africa

Islam

The countries of northwest Africa are together called the Maghrib. The region was once an important part of the Christian world but, well before the year 1000, the Mahgrib was invaded by Muslim armies from Arabia, and by the 11th century Muslim civilization was well established there.

Egypt, on the east of the Maghrib, was also Muslim. Gradually, through opening up trade routes and through people converting, Islam (the Muslim religion) spread southwards. Most of the early travellers in Africa were Muslims. Islamic culture was well developed and very learned, so during this time several excellent accounts were written by Muslims describing their travels.

A traditional mosque built in the city of Mopti in west Africa.

A 12th-century bowl from Egypt showing a priest of the Coptic Church.

Tribal Religions

The rest of Africa was generally based on tribal societies. Their religions were part of their daily life. They generally believed in one chief god, but also in magical powers. They associated these powers with animals and natural objects. They also believed that the spirits of their dead ancestors were with them, helping and advising, as well as judging their behaviour. It was therefore very important to them to pay proper respect to the ancestor spirits, often offering them lavish gifts.

Christianity

A Christian sect, the Coptic Church, spread from Egypt into Ethiopia in around the 4th century. During the 7th century the Arab invasions brought Islam to most of northern Africa, but the Coptic Church in Ethiopia remained strong, and survives to this day. Unlike other peoples, the Copts believe that Jesus has one nature, blending his human and divine sides. Other Christians say that his divine self and his human self are separate.

69

Japan

In 858 the Fujiwara, the leading noble family in Japan, rose to power, and ruled the country for the next 300 years. Michinaga (966–1028) was the greatest Fujiwara leader. Under his rule Japanese culture – particularly its literature – flourished.

Government, however, grew weaker under the Fujiwara. It became very corrupt, and as a result the country was divided up between lords who owned large amounts of land. Local warriors banded together for protection, and by the mid-12th century two clans, the Taira and the Minamoto, were the strongest. In 1160 the Taira crushed the Minamoto and then seized power from the Fujiwara. Twenty-five years later the Minamoto clan seized power from the Taira and established the first shogunate in Japan.

Yoritomo, the first of the Japanese *shoguns*, or military leaders, who ruled Japan for 700 years.

Sei Shonagon (966–about 1013)

Sei Shonagon was the daughter of a poet, and through her clever wit and intelligence got a job in the Japanese court of the empress Sadako in 991. Between 991 and 1000 she wote a diary, called the *Pillow Book,* that recounts her impressions and observations of court life. It is famous for its descriptions of nature and everyday life and is considered a classic of Japanese literature. Much of what we know about Japanese court life around this time is based on her writings.

Tea Ceremony

The Japanese tea ceremony is a special way of entertaining guests and follows a strict order. The ceremony takes place in a special building or room of a house. The host first brings in the utensils used to serve the tea, then offers sweets to the guests, then prepares and pours out the tea, then clears away the tea things. Zen Buddhist monks brought the idea of the tea ceremony back from China, drinking tea to help them stay awake during their long periods of meditation.

The Japanese tea ceremony is a long-established tradition that is still practised in Japan today.

Shoguns and *Samurais*

Although there was still an emperor, the real power was in the hands of the *shogun,* a hereditary military leader who ruled Japan. Shogun means commander in chief of all of the armed forces. Minamoto Yoritomo (1147–1199), a warrior and leader of the Minamoto clan, became the first shogun in 1192. His government was named the Kamakura shogunate after the city he chose as his capital. Although he was descended from royal blood, he was impatient with all of the traditional ceremonies in the court and concentrated more on governing and warfare. He was jealous and cold-hearted, but proved to be a strong and capable leader. Shoguns ruled Japan almost continuously for the next 700 years, and the country suffered frequent civil wars during this time.

A *samurai* was a warrior who worked for a *daimyo* (a lord who owned a large amount of land), under the shogun. The samurai made up their own class of people and wore two swords as a symbol of their status. They lived by a strict code of behaviour that was later called *bushido,* which means 'the way of the warrior'. A samurai was expected to be strong and brave in battle, and above all to be loyal to his daimyo, even over his own parents. In his daily life he was expected to be kind and honest and to live simply.

Izumi Tadahira, one of the great warriors of 12th-century Japan.

Zen Buddhism

Buddhists aim to find an inner sense of peace, beyond suffering and beyond life and death. Zen Buddhists believe that they can achieve this peace through a highly disciplined form of meditation, or thinking. Japanese monks who studied in China brought Zen Buddhism back to Japan in the late 12th and early 13th centuries, and it is still a very important religion in Japan today.

Rise of the Mongols

During the 13th century a vast empire was created that covered most of Asia and extended into eastern Europe. It was as big as any empire in history. It belonged to the Mongols, a nomadic (wandering) people who lived on the steppes (grasslands) of Mongolia.

The Tribes Unite

Before the 13th century the people of the Mongolian steppes were divided into rival tribes, each with its own leader. There was almost constant warfare between the tribes.

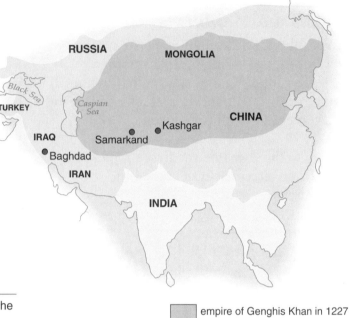

empire of Genghis Khan in 1227

greatest extent of Mongol empire

A Chinese painting showing Genghis Khan, the founder of the Mongol Empire, out hunting with a falcon.

Genghis Khan (about 1162–1227)

Genghis Khan, originally named Temujin, was born in around 1162 and came from a long line of tribal chiefs. He was only nine years old when his father was poisoned by a band of Tartars, another nomadic people of the steppes. Traditionally the chief's eldest son took over as ruler, but the tribe thought Temujin was too young and chose another as leader. Temujin and his family were abandoned by the tribe, and for years they endured terrible poverty and hunger.

As he grew older, Temujin's warrior spirit, ambition, and genius helped him become a great ruler among the Mongols. After many years of tribal wars, Temujin successfully defeated his greatest rivals. In 1206, when Temujin was about 39 years old, the Mongol tribes gathered together and declared him as their one and only ruler. It was then that he was named Genghis Khan, which probably means 'universal ruler'.

This changed in 1206 when, for the first time, the tribes united under one ruler – Genghis Khan. Under his brilliant leadership the mighty Mongol empire was created. With a ruthless army of skilled and powerful warriors, Genghis first invaded northern China and then swept across the rest of mainland Asia. He destroyed towns and cities, killing the terrified people who lived there. Although the Mongols could be very brutal, they were not uncontrollable warriors. Their army was highly organized, with generals who were fiercely loyal to Genghis. His soldiers were expert horsemen and archers and were extremely disciplined.

Genghis Khan is shown here seated surrounded by some of his generals.

Laws and Beliefs

As the empire grew, Genghis Khan created a set of laws called the Yasa. The government of the empire was based on these laws, and those who disobeyed the Yasa received a terrible punishment. Traditionally Mongol khans (rulers) were tolerant towards the customs and beliefs of other nations, and Genghis had in his government Muslim and Chinese advisers. The Muslim advisers taught Genghis that, instead of destroying the towns and cities he conquered, he could make use of their wealth and persuade their people to help run his empire. Despite Genghis Khan's brutality towards his enemies, those who agreed to his rule were treated fairly and were allowed to keep their own religions and lifestyles.

What did Genghis Khan Achieve?

In 1227 Genghis Khan died, undefeated in war. After his death, one of his sons, Ogadai, became the new khan. The Mongol empire stayed strong and united under Ogadai and his successors. They added European Russia,

Invasion of Khwarezm

In 1218 Genghis Khan's attention was drawn to an event in the empire of Khwarezm in central Asia. Muslim merchants, under the protection of Genghis, had travelled into a Khwarezm city to trade, but were put to death by the city's governor. Genghis was furious when he heard of this, and sent two ambassadors to the shah (ruler) of Khwarezm, demanding that the governor be turned over to him. The shah, thinking that the Mongols were unimportant, ordered the murder of the ambassadors. This so outraged Genghis that he declared war and invaded Khwarezm, destroying many cities and massacring their inhabitants. In one city, called Menz, a million people were slaughtered. The terrified shah fled to an island in the Caspian Sea, where he later died.

Turkey, Iran, and Iraq to the list of Mongol conquests. Although Genghis died long before the empire was complete, he left a kingdom so vast it would take almost six months to ride from one end to the other. Because this incredible empire was built in just 20 years, Genghis Khan is considered by many to be the greatest general and conqueror in history.

Kublai Khan

Most of Asia in the 13th century was ruled by the Mongols, a fierce nomadic (wandering) people from the grasslands of Mongolia. The first khan or ruler of the Mongols was Genghis Khan, who came to power in 1206. When he died in 1227, his family continued to expand the empire. In 1260 his grandson, Kublai (ruled 1260–1294), became khan. Kublai lived in northern China, then part of the Mongol empire, and his main ambition was to conquer the rest of China.

At that time the south of China was ruled by the Chinese Song dynasty, which had ruled the whole of China until 1127. Kublai's armies battled with the Song for several years until, in 1279, the Mongols triumphed and Kublai became the first Mongol emperor of China. After 150 years of being divided, China was again united under one dynasty, the Yuan, or Mongol dynasty. To help him rule a huge country like China, Kublai employed many experienced advisers. Among them were a number of foreigners, including the Italian explorer Marco Polo.

Under Kublai's rule, the Chinese population was divided into four categories.

Under the leadership of Kublai Khan the Mongol Empire reached its greatest extent.

Chinese Inventions

The Chinese were great inventors, and Marco Polo saw many things in China that were unknown in Europe. One of them was a black powder that exploded when lit – gunpowder – that the Chinese used to make fireworks for celebrations. China also had paper money, which seemed ridiculous to Europeans, who used only coins at that time. According to legend on his return to Italy, Marco Polo brought back a Chinese food made from flour and water and cut into thin strips. It was later adopted by the Italians, who named it pasta.

Fireworks, which are now used in celebrations throughout the world, were originally a Chinese invention.

The Mongols were skilled horsemen and fierce warriors.

The top two categories did not include any Chinese people. At the top were the Mongols, who were a tiny minority; the second category were the foreign government members; the third was made up of the wealthy Chinese people; the fourth, and by far the largest, category contained the peasants. All Chinese people paid taxes to support Kublai and his government.

While Kublai ran China, other members of his family governed the rest of the empire. The Mongol princes who ruled the vast grasslands of Central Asia were angry with Kublai because they felt he had abandoned his Mongol culture for that of China. Kublai was constantly fighting them to keep control of the empire.

Kublai Khan ruled China until his death in 1294. Other Mongol emperors followed Kublai in China, but in 1368 the Chinese overthrew the Mongol reign and a new dynasty, called the Ming, began.

Why the Mongols Succeeded

Genghis Khan and his generals used superb battle tactics. Their armies, often separated by hundreds of miles, communicated using horseback riders carrying messages. The soldiers were brilliant horsemen, and could shoot arrows accurately while riding at full gallop. They had different types of arrows – some for piercing armour, some for setting fire to buildings, and some with whistles attached for signalling. The army could ride up to 160 kilometres (100 miles) each day, often with little food, and was extremely disciplined. The Mongols were ruthless in battle, and they slaughtered millions of people during their conquests.

Mongol archers carried different types of arrows for different purposes.

The Hundred Years' War Begins

What Caused the War?

In 1337 war broke out between England and France. There were two main reasons why fighting started. Firstly, King Edward III of England (ruled 1327–1377) claimed that since his mother was the daughter of an earlier French king, Philip IV, the throne of France was rightfully his. Secondly, the kings of England had ruled parts of France since 1066, and the French were unhappy about this. Over the years they had retaken most of their land until only the regions of Gascony and Guienne in southwest France remained in English hands. Philip VI of France was determined to retake these too, as they were important winemaking areas.

The English wool trade with Flanders (modern Belgium) was also a target for Philip VI. The Flemish (the people of Flanders) saw that it was in their interest to protect the trade with England, from where they obtained the wool for their flourishing weaving industry. They therefore sided with Edward III. Philip decided to take back Gascony in 1337. Edward retaliated by sending support to the Flemish rebels and landing in northern France.

The Battle of Sluys in 1340 was a great victory for the English forces.

King Philip Hears a Riddle

After the Battle of Sluys nobody was brave enough to tell King Philip VI of France of his fleet's defeat. It was left to his jester, who told his master in the form of a riddle:

'Why are the English knights more cowardly than the French?'

'Because they did not jump in their armour into the sea like our brave Frenchmen'.

Sir John Froissart (1338–1401)

The events of Sluys and Crécy are known in some detail mainly because of the chronicles (historical accounts) written by a French knight, Sir John Froissart. Although a Frenchman, he was secretary to Edward III's wife and was a great admirer of the Black Prince. He wrote from first-hand knowledge, and we can be sure that the information that he recorded was reasonably accurate.

He declared himself King of France and the fighting began. It continued off and on until 1453 and became known as the Hundred Years' War.

Battle of Sluys

Edward III decided to take an army to Flanders in a large fleet of ships on 24 June 1340. Philip VI set out to stop this fleet at Sluys. Edward's ships attacked the French fleet, which was chained together to make it harder for the English to break through.

The English archers fired at the French, causing many casualties, and eventually broke the first line of ships. After more heavy fighting the English broke the second French line too. By the following morning Edward was victorious.

Battle of Crécy

For the next six years Edward III sent raiding parties into France. It was during one of these raids that the first land battle happened. Edward's force of 12,000 men was chased by a much larger French army and caught near Crécy on 26 August 1346. Edward chose a spot where his archers, armed with their deadly longbows, could do the most damage. The French attacked with their crossbowmen and then their mounted knights charged at the English soldiers. However, volley after volley of arrows fired by English longbowmen struck the French, causing terrible casualties.

Some French knights did reach the English lines and put the king's son, the Black Prince, in

The Black Prince's army attack the castle of Mortaigne.

The king of France meets his advisors at Sluys before the battle.

The Black Prince (1330–1376)

Edward, the Black Prince, was the eldest son of Edward III of England. He may have been given his nickname because he wore black armour in tournaments. He was just 16 when he was given command of one of his father's divisions at Crécy. At one stage he was surrounded by French knights. Messages for help were sent to his father, but the king dismissed the request with the words 'Let the boy win his spurs'. He was giving his son the opportunity to prove himself in battle, and if he did well he would be awarded a pair of gilt spurs, the customary reward to a young man who had become a knight. Edward was not prepared to favour anybody, not even his son!

danger, but they were driven off, leaving the English victorious. Edward returned home in 1347 where he prepared to renew the war. However the plague known as the Black Death was brought to England and many people died. This stopped Edward from continuing the war.

Law, Order, and Punishment

These 14th-century students are shown learning about law in a book from Venice.

The story of the outlaw Robin Hood has been popular for centuries. Actor Kevin Costner played the part of Robin in a recent film.

Henry II's New System of Law

Under the feudal system, every lord was the judge of the peasant farmers on his land. He always had the last say in any court case. However, in the 12th century, King Henry II (ruled 1154–1189) made many changes in English law. Instead of letting different lords or barons make up their own rules, he started a new system called common law, which was the same everywhere in the country.

Royal judges travelled around, holding trials in big towns for the worst crimes. This was a fairer system, although small crimes, such as the stealing of a pig, were still heard in local courts. Shire–reeves (chief magistrates) or sheriffs had to

Outlaws

People who did wrong but did not turn up in court were called outlaws. They had no rights for the rest of their life, and it was not a crime to kill them or steal from them. However, if someone thought he was wrongly accused, he could hide in a church. Here he would 'receive sanctuary', and no one was allowed to hurt him.

Many outlaws ran away to the forests, poaching the king's game and robbing travellers. The legend of Robin Hood and his 'merry men' is probably based on true stories about such outlaws.

Many punishments were very harsh. A law passed by Henry II in 1176 said that thieves had to have a hand and a foot cut off, then would be banished – forced to leave England for ever – with all they owned going to the king. Another cruel punishment was blinding. Barons had dungeons in their castles and kept enemies locked up for years, sometimes going away and letting them slowly starve to death. But putting people in prison was rare.

Death by beheading, being burnt alive, or hanging in the gallows, was the punishment for serious crimes like murder. However, even stealing more than a shilling was considered a serious crime! The torture of being hung, drawn, and quartered was used as an extra warning for crimes like treason (plotting against or disobeying the king).

Being placed in the pillory was a common punishment for minor offences in medieval times.

People who had committed small crimes, like begging or cheating in the market, could be flogged (whipped), or put in the stocks. The stocks, or pillory, were used to embarrass wrong-doers in a public place. Women who scolded their husbands might be shamed on the ducking stool. This involved tying the woman onto a stool and ducking her into a pond.

keep law and order in each county. It was their job to catch criminals and put them in prison until the king's judges arrived.

Trial by Ordeal

An old practice that was still used during Henry II's time was the trial by ordeal. This was a cruel test that people believed showed whether a person was guilty or innocent in the eyes of God. In the ordeal by fire, the accused person was forced to walk a short distance with a piece of red-hot iron in his or her hand. A bandage would be put on the burned hand for three days, and then taken off. If the burn was healing up the person would be declared innocent. Another test was ordeal by water. This time, the accused person was thrown into a pond. If the person sank, he or she was thought innocent and fished out of the water.

If the person floated, then it was thought that the devil was helping him or her, and the person must be guilty.

One other method to settle cases was trial by combat. Two people having an argument had to fight each other, and the one who lost the fight had to say he was in the wrong. Women and children or people too weak to fight could hire someone else called a champion to fight in their place.

The Normans introduced trial by jury to Britain in 1166. In this system a number of people gave a verdict regarding a person's innocence or guilt based on evidence. Trial by ordeal stopped in 1215 after the Pope stopped members of the clergy from participating. The jury system was greatly expanded after this and is still used today.

Sports, Toys, and Games

Fun and Games

Old pictures show us that medieval children played games that we still know today, like blind-man's buff, piggy-back, hide-and-seek, and bowls. A game like jacks was played by tossing the bones of a sheep off the back of the player's hand while trying to scoop up another bone from the floor. Kites and whip-tops were other favourite toys. People also enjoyed board games such as draughts and backgammon, and especially chess. Many people played

Arabs playing chess. Chess may have originated in India some time around the 7th century AD.

An early version of football was played along the streets of medieval towns.

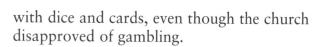

Peasants were sometimes given the chance to play 'futeball' (football) on their lord's land, with a ball made from a blown-up pig's bladder. Sometimes the pitch was miles long, because the goals were in different villages! There were no proper rules, so the game got wild and bloody. Children from rich families played football as well, and a kind of cricket using a curved stick called a cryc. They also played hockey, skittles, and a game like modern golf.

with dice and cards, even though the church disapproved of gambling.

In around 1100 young men in London exercised by jumping, throwing stones and javelins, and holding wrestling matches. When the rivers and lakes froze hard, people in northern Europe strapped animal shinbones to their feet and skated on the ice, using sticks to build up speed.

Mock Battles

War was a big part of medieval life, so many

80

With no television or cinema, people needed to provide their own entertainment. Feast days and festivals were religious holidays, but were often an excuse for merrymaking, with dancing, plays, and games. Wandering acrobats and jugglers performed their tricks in the market square or barons' castles, and contortionists twisted their bodies into strange shapes. There were also performing bears and monkeys, and a popular competition was to see who could catch a pig by its slippery tail. Cock fighting, bull-baiting, and even bear-baiting would always attract a crowd.

At some festivals peasants were allowed to play games that turned the tables on the lord. The lord might invite his workers into the manor house one day a year and treat them like noblemen, letting them eat, drink, and enjoy themselves at his expense.

Musicians and jugglers provide the entertainment in a 13th-century German castle.

The Thrill of the Chase

Hunting on horseback with dogs was a favourite pastime for rich people in the Middle Ages. From Norman times, about one fourth of the land in England was set aside as hunting preserves for the king and his nobles. This was called 'forest', whether or not there were any trees. Wild boar and wolves were still common in Britain then, and were hunted alongside hares and foxes. Ordinary people also liked to hunt or set snares, but could have their hands cut off for poaching in the king's forest! Rich men also used hawks and falcons to kill smaller birds in mid-air for fun and for food. Children played at hunting too, with sling shots or bows.

competitions were actually training for battle. Rich people held jousting tournaments, with teams of armed knights holding mock battles, while barons and ladies watched from wooden grandstands. Each contestant tried to knock his opponent off his horse as they rode at each other with lances. In another type of contest knights used swords and maces (spiked clubs). Sometimes, knights in full armour would fight for a lady's hand in marriage. Even though the weapons were blunt, men were often killed. Children of knights and barons would learn to fight using wooden swords and lances, aiming at targets called quintains.

Most young men were expected to practise

archery regularly, and archery competitions were often held. Because archers were so important to the English army, by the end of the 14th century Richard II tried to ban football, as it was taking so many young men away from their archery practice!

Medicine

In the Middle Ages people didn't understand how to protect themselves against diseases. Bones and leftover food were often thrown onto the rushes strewn over the floors of their houses. Toilets, if they existed, were emptied into the rivers, or even onto the streets! The thatch of houses was usually crawling with rats and insects. Drinking water was often dirty, and there wasn't enough clean water for washing.

There were few medicines that

A carving above a shop selling ointments and other medicines in 12th-century Italy.

Hospitals and Medical Schools

If people got ill, most of them would be cared for at home by their own families. Usually the only kind of hospital care was in monasteries or convents, where the monks or nuns would feed and look after patients, using herbal medicines from their gardens. From the 13th century people who wanted to practise medicine started going to the new medical schools, but there were still many untrained doctors. The first medical school in Europe was set up in the southern Italian town of Salerno, and this was followed by others in Italy and France. The doctors of Salerno put together a guide to health written as a long poem, and one of its most famous teachings was translated into English as:

'Use three physicians still: first Doctor Quiet, Next Doctor Merryman, and Doctor Diet.'

One of the few places for poor people to find medical care was in convents or monasteries.

did any good, and operations often ended in the death of the patient.

Only about one in every ten people in these times lived to be as old as 50. Poor diets caused diseases like scurvy and rickets, and a shortage of food when the harvests were bad made people more likely to die of other illnesses such as influenza.

In medieval times bleeding, or blood-letting, was thought to be a good way of curing some illnesses.

Arab Advances

In Muslim countries, medical and surgical ideas were far more advanced than in Europe. People returning from crusades brought back some of these useful ideas and customs. A great Arab doctor called Avicenna wrote a medical encyclopaedia which was used for many years by European doctors.

Common Cures

Doctors were expensive, so most people in a town would see the local apothecary (chemist) for advice. Apothecaries sold herbal remedies, tooth powders, and even magic potions. A recipe for an ointment that was meant to cure leprosy used the white of an egg and a unicorn's liver! A very popular way of deciding what disease patients had was to look carefully at the colour of their urine, and there were special charts with pictures to help figure out what was wrong.

Barbers acted as dentists and also did small operations. The red and white stripes on the barber's pole were a sign that he did blood-letting, which was thought to be an important way of helping people get better. Leeches were used to suck the blood, or a cut would be made in a vein in the arm. People could die from losing too much blood this way. Surgery was dangerous because there was a big risk that the wound would become infected. There were no proper anaesthetics to dull the pain, although alcohol and herbs were used. Some kinds of operation were very crude, for example amputations and trepanning – drilling a hole in the head! There were untrained people who specialized in pulling out rotten teeth.

Some cures were based on strange superstitions, for example the idea that the hand of a dead woman could cure cancer. People believed that praying to saints, touching a holy relic, going on a crusade, or even paying money to the church would help them get better.

Lepers

Everyone was afraid of leprosy, a disease that eats away at the flesh of the victim. Lepers were made to live apart in 'lazar houses', begging for a living, wearing special clothes, and carrying bells or clappers to warn people to get out of their way. By the end of the Middle Ages leprosy had mostly died out in Europe.

Birth

One medical job for women was to be a midwife and help mothers have their babies. Unfortunately, it was not unusual for the baby or the mother to die during childbirth. Sometimes an operation called a Caesarean section would be used to deliver the baby if the mother had already died in labour.

The Black Death

The Plague Comes to Europe

In 1347 a Mongol army was attacking a town called Kaffa in the Crimea, a peninsula on the northern shores of the Black Sea. Many of the Mongols were sick and dying from a terrible disease or plague that was spreading from the East.

The Mongol commander had an idea that was to have terrible consequences. Before giving up the siege of Kaffa he had the corpses of plague victims catapulted into the city. The disease soon broke out among the defenders of Kaffa.

In October 1347 ships belonging to merchants from Genoa arrived in the port of Messina in Sicily. They had sailed from Kaffa and had brought the plague with them. Soon afterwards ships carrying the infection arrived in Genoa as well. By January 1348 the plague reached the French port of Marseilles and began to spread through France. By the summer it had crossed the Channel into southern England.

Dreadful Death

Soon people everywhere were coming down with this strange and horrible illness. It would go from one house to another, and sometimes whole families or even villages were wiped out. There was no cure. To escape the deadly fever, people would pack up their belongings and hurry away to the countryside in an awful panic. Unfortunately, some of them were already infected, and they brought the plague with them to these out-of-the-way places.

As more and more people died, there were not enough healthy people to bury the dead or care for the dying. Doctors and priests did what little they could, although many were also terrified of getting the disease. Many victims' corpses were buried in huge open pits, or even burnt. On some ships the plague struck whole crews while they were at sea. One ship from England ran aground in Norway with only dead men aboard.

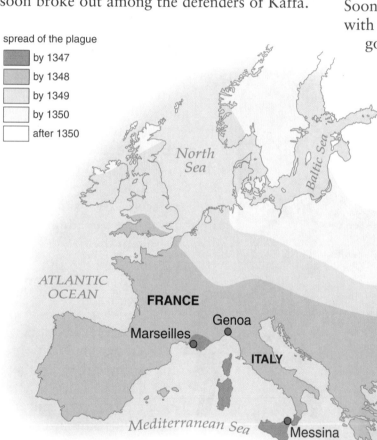

spread of the plague

- by 1347
- by 1348
- by 1349
- by 1350
- after 1350

How the Black Death spread across Europe

Possible Causes of the Plague

People racked their brains to try to figure out what was causing the plague. Was it bad air from the planets? Was it the punishment of God? Doctors from the University of Paris thought that the plague was caused by something in rainwater. First it was hoped that only wicked people caught the disease, but it soon became clear that both good and bad people died.

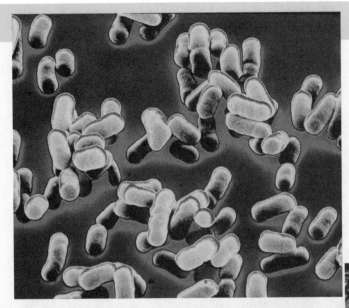

The real cause of the Black Death was not uncovered until 500 years afterwards when the bacterium *Yersinia pestis* was identified. This microbe lives in the stomachs of fleas and in the blood of rats on which the fleas live. It could be transmitted to humans by the bite of the infected flea. Rats from the ships that arrived in Messina and other ports soon joined the local rats, bringing infection with them. Sailors and merchants carried infected fleas on their clothing and bacteria in their bodies. In this way the disease spread rapidly, by rat, by flea, and on the breath of its human victims. It never occurred to the frightened people that it would help to drive out the rats.

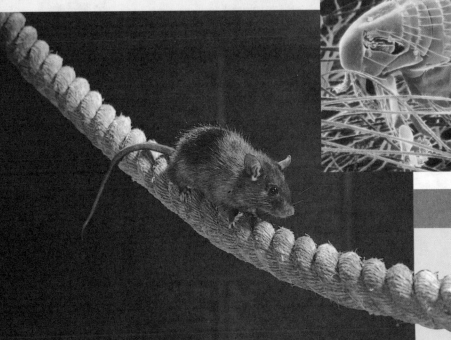

The cause of the plague: bacteria (above left) carried by fleas (above) that live on rats (left). When the fleas bit humans they passed on the deadly bacteria.

The Greatest Disaster

It was very hard to keep records of how many people died, but it seems that in the 14th century about 25 million people in Europe died of the plague – probably one-third of the whole population. For centuries after that smaller plagues continued to break out from time to time. The Black Death was one of the worst disasters in recorded history.

Two Kinds of Plague

There were two ways in which someone could fall victim to the plague. The first was to be bitten by an infected flea. This is called bubonic plague, because painful lumps called buboes appear on the victim's armpits, neck, and groin. Blackish patches also appear on the skin, caused by bleeding under the surface. This is why the plague is sometimes called the Black Death. People infected in this way usually die after five to ten days. A few lucky ones recover.

The second way to catch the plague was by breathing in infected particles sprayed on the breath of someone who has the disease. This is called pneumonic plague and it spreads like a cold or influenza, carried on coughs and sneezes. Pneumonic plague affects the lungs, causing chest pains and the coughing up of blood. The victim almost always dies after two to three days.

The Aztecs Come to Mexico

Some time in the 12th century a small, nomadic (wandering) group of tribal peoples arrived in a valley in central Mexico. According to their legends, they had wandered from a place called Aztlan, in northern Mexico. They were called the Mexica, or the Aztecs.

For a long time they remained poor, struggling to survive. They had to pay the peoples ruling the area high taxes, and the places they were allowed to live in at first were not fertile. They quickly became known for their brutality and lust for blood in battle. Because of this, they were driven out of kingdom after kingdom.

Eventually they settled and founded a state that became very powerful. In 1325 they built a great city, Tenochtitlán, on two islands in the middle of a lake.

Religion

The Aztecs had many gods. Their chief god was Huitzilopochtli. His name meant 'hummingbird on the left', and he was a god of war and also a sun god. Huitzilopochtli was the god of the city of Tenochtitlán.

War was central to the Aztecs' religious view of life. They believed war was the god's

The Aztec god Huitzilopochtli. Prisoners captured by Aztec warriors were sacrificed at the god's temple.

'marketplace' where he would obtain human beings to be sacrificed to him as food. Aztec sacrifices were cruel; they would hold the victim down, cut open his chest, and the chief priest would tear his heart out to give to the god. The body was then thrown down a great set of steps to the ground, where the legs and

86

Aztec Agriculture

The Mexica, or Aztecs, chose as their final settling place a valley ringed by mountains and studded with lakes. It was not easy to farm there. Much of the land was too high to be fertile. Any useful land was on steep slopes, or waterlogged. The Aztecs found ways of tackling these difficulties. They built terraces on the mountainside. Terraces are pieces of land made level, with vertical drops from one level to the next, like giant shallow steps. This is a way of preventing the precious water from running down the mountain away from the crops. They also dug ditches along the terraces to carry water easily. They used ditches also to carry water down into the valleys where they lived. They even managed to convert part of the biggest lake, Texcoco, from salt water to fresh water.

Their most spectacular farming technique was the use of the *chinampa.* This was a way of creating fertile land in swampy areas, or even in a lake. It had been in use in the valley area for some time before the Aztecs arrived there, but they perfected the system and used it more extensively than anyone had done before. They built large rafts of straw on which they placed river mud. They planted trees and vegetables so that their long roots anchored the rafts to the bottom of the lake. They built fences around the edges of the rafts to keep the mud in. By placing the rafts (*chinampas*) a little way apart they created a system of canals throughout their city.

The Aztecs were skilled farmers as well as warriors, growing crops such as corn and tomatoes in raised fields called chinampas. They kept journals that helped them determine the best times for planting and harvesting.

arms were cut off. The Aztecs would then eat part of the body as a religious ritual, joining their god in his meal. Although this practice was brutal, many of those sacrificed felt honoured, even excited, at going to join the gods.

The Aztecs also worshipped the sun as Tonatiuh, a god who was the source of life. They were convinced that if this god was not fed regularly with human hearts the sun would no longer rise and bring light, warmth, and new life. This ensured that they kept up the bloody habit of human sacrifice, increasing the number of victims as their civilization grew.

The Incas

The Founding of the Inca State

Inca legend tells that a hero, Manco Capac, came with his people from Lake Titicaca, on the border between modern Peru and Bolivia, north to the valley of Cuzco, high in the Andes Mountains. There he stuck into the earth a golden stick he carried, and founded the Inca state.

This may or may not be true, but from about 1200 the Inca people did settle in the valley of Cuzco, and quickly conquered many of the neighbouring peoples. By the 16th century the Inca empire reached from Ecuador to Chile.

Transport and Communications

Two roads ran right along the Inca empire. Other roads crossed them. These brilliantly built roads totalled 16,000 kilometres (10,000 miles) in length. Although the Incas had roads, they didn't have the wheel so they had to travel on foot with Llamas carrying goods. Positioned along the roads were messenger-posts. A messenger would run from one post to the next, carrying information on quipus. A quipu was a set of knotted cords. The knots and colours of the cords stored coded facts and figures. Quipus were vital in keeping records.

Part of the walls of the Inca fortress of Sacsahuaman, near their capital, Cuzco.

Llamas like these were essential to the Incas' way of life.

Llamas and Eating Habits

Llamas were essential to the Inca way of life. They were used to carry goods, and for their warm wool. Their manure was used to fertilize the fields, and occasionally their meat was eaten. More often the Inca ate the meat of wild animals such as deer, rabbits, and *guanaco* – a kind of wild llama.

The Inca also ate potatoes and another root crop, called oca. A grain called quinoa was very common. In lowland areas, maize (sweetcorn) was grown. Maize flour was used for making bread, porridge, and beer.

In this Inca ceremony a herd of llamas is offered to the sun god, Inti.

Inca Society

Inca society was very well organized. The empire was divided into four provinces, or quarters. Each quarter was divided into sub-provinces of 10,000 households each. Each sub-province was divided into groups of 100 each, and again into groups of 10. There was an official in charge of each group, at each level. These officials were the nobility, and above them all was the king, or Sapa Inca. The Inca believed that the king was the son of the sun god, Inti. He had to marry his sister, who was called the Caya.

Most people were farmers, but everyone had to do some work regularly for the whole kingdom. To organize this work, people were divided into 12 groups, according to age. Jobs were allotted according to the abilities of the different age groups. All the work necessary for the efficient running of the kingdom was done in this way, under the direction of nobles who ran the groups.

Sacrifice

To make sure of the friendship of both gods and spirits, the Inca made sacrifices to them. Usually, they sacrificed animals, and also gave them precious things like beautiful cloth, as well as beer made from maize. Unlike the Aztecs, who sacrificed thousands of people every year, the Inca sacrificed people only at the coronation of a new Sapa Inca.

Religion

The Incas worshipped several gods. Their chief god was Inti, the sun god. His wife was Mama Quilla, the moon. Then there was Pacha Mama, the earth. Illapa was the storm god, bringing messages from the sun. Viracocha was the god who had created everything.

Holy places, called huacas, were important to the Inca. Huacas could be caves, rocks, springs, or other special spots. They believed spirits lived in the huacas. Many of the spirits were, the Inca believed, their ancestors. These could be animals, plants, or even rocks.

Index

Picture Acknowledgements

t = top, b = bottom, l = left, r = right

4 et archive; 5 British Library/AKG London; 6 Erich Lessing/AKG London; 7 t Michael Dent/Impact, b et archive; 8 t British Library/et archive, b Musée de la Tapisserie, Bayeux/Michael Holford; 9 Musée de la Tapisserie, Bayeux/Erich Lessing/AKG London; 10–11 t British Library/et archive, b Bridgeman Art Library; 12 Biblioteca Estense, Modena/et archive; 12–13 Rheinisches Landesmuseum, Bonn/et archive; 13 et archive; 14–15 English Heritage; 16 l National Library of Scotland/Bridgeman Art Library, r et archive; 17 t Michael St Maur Sheil/Collections, b Roy Rainford/Robert Harding; 18 British Library/et archive; 19 t Bürgerbibliothek, Bern/AKG London, b British Library/et archive; 20–21 Ancient Art & Architecture Collection; 22 Musée de Cluny/et archive; 23 t British Library, b Steve Parry/Impact; 24 AKG London; 25 Stadtmuseum Aachen/et archive, b et archive; 26 AKG London; 26–27 Archives Nationales, Paris/et archive; 27 Santa Croce, Florence/et archive; 28 Skyscan Photolibrary; 29 t Adam Woolfitt/Robert Harding, b Museo dell'Opera del Duomo, Florence/et archive; 30 University Library, Heidelberg/et archive; 31 et archive; 32–33 t Biblioteca Marciana, Venice/et archive, b University Library, Heidelberg/et archive; 34 Bibliothèque Nationale, Paris/et archive; 35 t British Library/et archive, b Biblioteca Marciana, Venice/et archive; 36 University Library, Heidelberg/et archive; 37 t British Library/et archive, b University Library, Heidelberg/et archive; 38 Bibliothèque Nationale, Paris/et archive; 39 Giraudon/Bridgeman Art Library; 40 Ancient Art & Architecture Collection; 41 et archive; 43 t Christie's Images, b National Palace Museum, Taiwan/et archive; 44 Mark Henley/Impact; 45 t Tom Webster/Impact, b Ancient Art & Architecture Collection; 46 l National Museum of New Delhi/Angelo Hornak, r Victoria & Albert Museum/Bridgeman Art Library; 47 David Cumming/Eye Ubiquitous; 48 l Museum of Mankind/Bridgeman Art Library, r National Museum of New Zealand/Werner Forman Archive; 49 National Museum of New Zealand/Werner Forman Archive; 50 t Maxwell Museum of Anthropology, New Mexico/Werner Forman Archive, b Bridgeman Art Library; 51 Werner Forman Archive; 52 et archive; 53 t Bibliothèque Nationale, Paris/et archive, b Bibliothèque de l'Arsenal, Paris/et archive; 54–55 British Museum/et archive; 55 Bibliothèque de l'Arsenal, Paris/et archive; 56 Christ Church, Oxford/et archive; 57 t British Library /Bridgeman Art Library, b Bibliothèque Nationale, Paris/et archive; 58 t British Library/et archive, b et archive; 59–60 British Library/et archive; 61–63 Bibliothèque Nationale, Paris/Bridgeman Art Library; 64 et archive; 65 British Library/et archive; 66 G Buthaud/Impact; 67 Julian Calder/Impact; 68 Robert Aberman; 69 t David Reed/Impact, b Victoria & Albert Museum/Bridgeman Art Library; 70 National Museum, Tokyo/AKG London, b Pushkin Museum, Moscow/Bridgeman Art Library; 71 School of Oriental & African Studies, London/ Bridgeman Art Library; 72 AKG London; 73 Bibliothèque Nationale, Paris/AKG London; 74 t AKG London, b Ed Pritchard/Tony Stone; 75 t Edinburgh University Library/et archive, b AKG London; 76 Bibliothèque Nationale, Paris/et archive; 77 British Library/et archive; 78 t Biblioteca Marciana, Venice/et archive, b Ronald Grant Archive; 79 Bibliothèque Nationale, Paris/et archive; 80 t Escorial/ Michael Holford, b Mary Evans Picture Library; 81 Mary Evans Picture Library; 82 t Museo Civico, Modena/et archive, b AKG London; 83 British Library/et archive; 85 t Eye of Science/Science Photo Library, bl Stephen Dalton/Natural History Photographic Agency, br Dr Tony Brain/Science Photo Library; 86 et archive; 87 l Helen W Price/Oxford Scientific Films, r Zig Leszczynski/Oxford Scientific Films; 88 t Stuart Wilson/Eye Ubiquitous, b Doug Allan/Oxford Scientific Films; 89 et archive.

Cover illustrations (clockwise from top right):
British Library/et archive; Rheinisches Landesmuseum, Bonn/et archive; British Library/AKG London; English Heritage; English Heritage

Every effort has been made to give the correct acknowledgement for each picture. However, should there be any inaccuracy or omission, we would be pleased to insert the correct acknowledgement in a future edition or printing of this volume.